LOCKED IN
A VIOLENT
EMBRACE

Sage Series on Violence Against Women

Series Editors

Claire M. Renzetti
St. Joseph's University

Jeffrey L. Edleson
University of Minnesota

In this series . . .

LOCKED IN A VIOLENT EMBRACE

Understanding and Intervening in Domestic Violence

Zvi Eisikovits
Eli Buchbinder

SVAW

Sage Series on Violence Against Women

Sage Publications, Inc.
International Educational and Professional Publisher
Thousand Oaks ▪ London ▪ New Delhi

For information:

Sage Publications, Inc.
2455 Teller Road
Thousand Oaks, California 91320
E-mail: order@sagepub.com

Sage Publications Ltd.
6 Bonhill Street
London EC2A 4PU
United Kingdom

Sage Publications India Pvt. Ltd.
M-32 Market
Greater Kailash I
New Delhi 110 048 India

Printed in the United States of America

Library of Congress Cataloging-in-Publication Data

Eisikovits, Zvi.
  Locked in a violent embrace: Understanding and intervening in domestic violence / by Zvi Eisikovits, Eli Buchbinder.
      p. cm. — (Sage series on violence against women)
  Includes bibliographical references and index.
  ISBN 0-7619-0538-3 (cloth : alk. paper)
  ISBN 0-7619-0539-1 (pbk.: alk. paper)
  1. Wife abuse—Israel. 2. Abused women—Israel—Interviews. 3.
Abusive men—Israel—Interviews. 4. Abused women—Counseling
of—Israel. 5. Abusive men—Counseling of—Israel. I. Buchbinder, Eli.
II. Title. III. Series.
  HV6626.23.I75 E57 2000
  362.82'927'095694—dc21   00-008366

This book is printed on acid-free paper.

00   01   02   03   04   05   06   7   6   5   4   3   2   1

Acquisition Editor:	C. Terry Hendrix
Editorial Assistant:	Kris Lundquist
Production Editor:	Sanford Robinson
Editorial Assistant:	Victoria Cheng
Typesetter:	Lynn Miyata
Indexer:	Teri Greenberg
Cover Designer:	Michelle Lee

Contents

To our partners and children
Rivka, Goldi, Nir, and Lotem

Foreword

By the early 1970s it was clear that decades of inattention was about to give way to a more open and public discourse about violence in intimate relationships. I recall that when my first book, *The Violent Home*, was reviewed by Erin Pizzey (author of *Scream Quietly or the Neighbors Will Hear*), Pizzey opened her review by suggesting that "those concerned with any form of social caring should empty their bookshelves to make space for a massive onslaught of literature on this subject" (*Nursing Mirror*, January 29, 1976). Pizzey underestimated how big the onslaught would be. Books on violence between men and women overflow bookcases, not merely bookshelves.

The social transformation of what is now referred to as "domestic violence" or "violence toward women" was facilitated by what was, at least initially, a symbiotic relationship between feminist advocates and social scientists. Grassroots advocates, like Erin Pizzey (who declined to label herself a "feminist") established shelters, spearheaded class action suits against police and prosecutors, and fought for legislation that protected women from intimate and private abuse. Advocates had to overcome initial indifference and then active backlash, especially a pervasive victim blaming that argued that the best solution to the problem of domestic violence would be for the women to simply leave their batterers.

Social scientists provided the descriptive data that violence toward women was much more widespread than anyone, especially the victims and advocates, had imagined. Social scientists also provided data and evidence that undermined myths and conventional wisdoms clouding the reality of violence toward women, including the myth that women can simply leave abusive relationships.

LOCKED IN A VIOLENT EMBRACE

Ultimately, a cleavage developed between advocates and social scientists. To somewhat oversimplify, the cleavage seemed to begin when social scientists, including Murray Straus, Suzanne Steinmetz, and myself, reported that there were high rates of female-to-male violence as well as high rates of male-to-female violence in intimate relationships. Media accounts of our results (and many of our own publications) proposed that female-to-male violence was as common as male-to-female violence. Such a finding was an anathema to advocates because it undercut their efforts to place violence toward women on the national policy agenda as a major social and health problem.

The cleavage widened over theoretical explanations. Social scientists and advocates rejected intra-individual explanations—battering could not be explained solely on the basis of individual psychopathology and remaining with a battering partner was certainly not an indication that a woman was a masochist. Social scientists developed theories of the middle range to explain violence toward women—drawing on social psychological research on aggression, criminological research, and research on family conflict. Evidence to support such theoretical framing was often derived from survey data, including national surveys and local surveys of college students. Advocates, including a growing number of women social scientists such as Kristi Yllö, Rebecca Dobash, and Mildred Pagelow, conceptualized violence toward women from a macro-level. Violence toward women was explained as one manifestation of male coercive control of women. "The patriarchy" was the core conceptual construct that explained the abuse and control of women. Positivist research was a manifestation of the patriarchy and thus, results that found high rates of female-to-male violence was part of the pattern of coercive control of women.

For much of the next two decades, social scientists and advocates labored in separate camps (with the exception of feminist social scientists). While they claimed to have the same goals, the two groups often clashed, and rarely spoke to one another in civil tones. Positivist social scientists continued to carry out surveys and often found that such surveys produced results that were contrary to claimsmaking by advocates and advocacy researchers. Feminist researchers pursued lines of research designed to empower victims of battering and that focused more broadly on the social-cultural factors that suppressed and victimized women.

Somewhere in the process of the social transformation of domestic violence from a personal trouble to a social problem, the actual personal trouble was obscured and lost. While social scientists and advocates succeeded beyond expectations in defining domestic violence as a social problem and securing a place for domestic violence on the policy agenda, the actual personal trouble faded into the background.

Zvi Eisikovits and Eli Buchbinder have returned the focus to the personal trouble with their book *Locked in a Violent Embrace*. Their analysis is controversial in many ways. First, using qualitative methods, they find that examining men beating women alone will not provide a rounded picture concerning the phenomenology of violence. Second, they focus on violent relationships that do not result in the termination of the marriage. Women are struck, women are beaten, and the man and woman continue to remain together as a couple.

What is unique and useful about *Locked in a Violent Embrace* is that Eisikovits and Buchbinder examine the most common form of intimate violence, men and women hitting and hurting one another and yet remaining together. Over the last thirty years, in an effort to convince an apathetic public that violence in the home was a serious social problem, advocates, social scientists, and the media tended to focus on the most severe and troubling forms of intimate violence. Obviously, such violence is merely the tip of the iceberg. Less obvious is that the policies and programs designed to deal with the iceberg's tip may be not be appropriate for the largest portion of the iceberg below the policy surface.

Locked in a Violent Embrace is unique on another level. The data come from qualitative interviews conducted in Israel, yet the authors bring to their writing much cross-cultural experience from other places such as the U.S. and Europe. Thus Eisikovits and Buchbinder uncover not just the everyday patterns and entrapment of violent relationships, but also the universal features of intimate violence.

The new century offers the opportunity to develop a more mature and holistic understanding of intimate violence. The successes of the last three decades are ready to be consolidated. Already there are signs that bridges are being made. Advocates and positivist social scientists are talking again and working together. Both need to remember that progress with resolving the social problem can only be achieved by understanding the nature of the personal trouble—those locked in the violent embrace.

—Richard J. Gelles
Joanne and Raymond Welsh Chair of
Child Welfare and Family Violence
Co-Director, Center for the Study of Youth Policy
Co-Director, Center for Children's Policy, Practice, and Research
School of Social Work, University of Pennsylvania

Acknowledgments

This book is of our own making, and thus we are solely responsible for its contents. However, in many ways, it is the result of a collective effort by a group of talented and dedicated people, known in Israel as The University of Haifa Research Group on Intimate Violence, who have worked with us over the years on various projects. Their ideas, insights, and feedback are present throughout this book, to such an extent that we often consider our own thinking to be the result of this fruitful synthesis.

We wish to extend our special thanks to Ruchama Gusinsky for her extraordinary commitment to this project and for her help in making it into a reality. Her knowledge, sensitivity, and commitment, as well as her reflective ability added depth to our endeavor. We thank Zeev Winstok for his sharpness in helping to analyze mountains of complex qualitative data, reduce it to manageable size, and often, represent it graphically in an intelligible fashion. Our thanks go to Hadas Goldblatt and Dalit Yassour for helping us analyze the data for the chapters on accounts and on emotions, respectively.

We thank the series editors, Professor Claire Renzetti and Professor Jeffrey Edleson, for making this book possible and for their patient and highly professional comments on earlier drafts of this book. We want to express our gratitude to Professor Rivka Eisikovits whose incisive criticisms on the conceptual aspects of the book added much coherence to the final product.

Our language editor, Mr. Yoram Navon, confronted us with the difficulties of writing in a language not our own and joined with us on the difficult journey of trying to create some measure of correspondence between what we meant and what we wrote. If the final product is more readable, it is because of his contribution.

We thank the Harry Frank Guggenheim Foundation for supporting the initial stages of the project and also Professor Edleson for his partnership throughout this project.

We thank the men and women who were our informants and shared with us their lives and hardships, opened their homes, and allowed us to come close to the ways they understood the experiences of intimate violence. Last, we thank our families and children for their patience and support throughout this project. We dedicate this book to our partners and thank them for fulfilling lives in which we have never known the meaning of violence.

1

Introduction

Constructing the Script

A man beats a woman. A woman is beaten by a man. A man and a woman live in violence, and yet they remain together, they view themselves as a couple.

The present book undertakes the task of describing and analyzing the experience of dyadic life in violence. It focuses on couples who choose to remain together in spite of violence, trying to make sense out of a life in the shadow of pain, terror, guilt, and humiliation. It is an attempt to understand a life that often seems unlivable, hell-like.

Chapters 2, 3, and 4 describe and analyze the development of violent events, behavior, and relationship patterns in its aftermath and the daily realities in the intervals between violent events. Chapters 5 and 6 examine the emotions and metaphors woven into the joint life of violence. Chapter 7 presents the accounts of violent events used by couples with the intent of presenting a convincing normative image to their audiences. Chapter 8 explores the implications of exposure to various social control agents and examines the extent to which such normative expectations are met. In Chapter 9, we attempt to translate the understanding accumulated throughout the book into a series of guidelines for intervention.

We have painstakingly gained our understanding through data accumulated over the past 12 years, in a series of qualitative studies, in clinical practice with batterers and battered women, and as champions of the cause of battered women. We developed a large database of semistructured in-depth interviews, structured observations, life histories, and case studies of battered women and men who battered. More specifically, our data collection started with a relatively large study funded by the Harry Frank Guggenheim Foundation from 1986 to 1990 (Eisikovits & Edleson, 1986). The study employed a mixed quantitative-qualitative design, which yielded qualitative data obtained from 80 in-depth interviews with 40 couples, wherein the men perpetually committed violence against the women and the couple remained together. Additional data was collected from later studies, more limited in scope, which explored specific aspects of the microcosm of cohabitant partners who experienced violence and the multiple ways in which they gave meaning to their joint lives. This subset of data was composed of 60 in-depth interviews with 30 couples. The topics ranged from the individual perceptions of violent events by batterers and battered women to experiencing everyday reality as a family living in the shadow of violence, as well as relationships with broader social systems that became part of the participants' attempts to cope with the violence. A study of police handling of intimate violence, funded by the Ministry of Internal Security in Israel, enabled us to collect data about batterers' and battered women's perception of police intervention. This kind of cumulative data allowed us to use understandings acquired in one study as the context for analyzing the data in subsequent ones.

Our work progressed over time from the descriptive-analytic to the theoretical model-building levels. Throughout this process, it was particularly enriching and rewarding to develop a reflective practice model that served as the basis for the establishment of the first research and practice unit in Israel for intervention with battered women and perpetrators of violence. This allowed for continuous testing of our emerging ideas in light of the experiences of our clients in a rapidly changing sociopolitical climate. In it, intimate violence in Israel was transformed from an individual and interpersonal problem to a social ill. Our research and practice over the years exposed us to battered women and batterers from various ethnic and cultural backgrounds (both Ashkenazi Jews—of Eastern European and North American origin—and Sephardic Jews—of North African and Middle Eastern origin) with diverse education and income levels. Whereas most of our informants were middle or lower middle class, there was wide variation within this group. They ranged in age from their early 20s to their late 50s and had from one to seven children. They lived in violence for periods ranging from several months to three decades. We studied battered women and batterers in a variety of life situations, couples who remained together and couples who parted, women living in shelters and living alone in the community. In this book, we address the populations of those who chose to remain together in violence. They were the overwhelming majority of our informants.

Throughout the book, we illustrate our understanding of the informant's point of view through quotation and commentary. The quotes are illustrations of experiential patterns that aim to bridge the distance between a general conceptual category and specific experiences in order to bring life to the abstractions. The attempt to view the quotes as "representative" of a category is both simplistic and misleading. Just as in the case of the statistical mean's phantom, such so-called representative quotes are nonexistent. This is because under any given conceptual category, there are an infinite number of specific situations. The meaning of concepts such as loss of trust (in Chapter 2) or order and disorder (in Chapter 4) are constructed from very different life events. Similarly, the events that constitute the ritual by which violence is transformed from specific occurrences to a way of life (Chapter 2) are highly divergent among couples and within the same couple over time. The quotes are given to highlight the similarities rather than the differences within a conceptual category. We have no intention of blurring the boundaries between the specific and the general in our interview data. On the contrary, these boundaries need to be taken into account when the reader crosses them. Confusion may be fostered by the fact that we work with the quotes beyond the descriptive-illustrative level and often perform thematic in-depth analysis aimed to capture various levels of meaning. The quotes represent a concept but not the entire range of situations from which we created them.

Although attempting to adhere to the technical procedures of qualitative content analysis and the ethical precautions entailed, our interpretations reflect our own views, philosophy, and experiences concerning the issues under scrutiny. Perhaps, this is because whenever we attempt to reconstruct another person's life experiences, we project our own. In addition, there is the issue of "official" versus the "subjective" realities of woman battering (Loseke, 1987). There is always tension and discrepancy between professional discourse, which is formal, typified, and objectified, and the participant's perspective, which is personal, experiential, and subjective. We are also tainted by this official discourse, but we tried to remain acutely aware of this double reality and to bracket it out whenever possible, to keep as close as possible to the subjective perspectives of our informants. We also sought to promote an ongoing dialectic between the official and subjective perspectives while making the boundaries between the two explicit. Taking all this into account, we believe that we have been able to reflect, to a high degree of accuracy, the inner world of people living in violence.

The lives of the people we studied always circle around violence. It never disappears nor is it forgotten, but its relative focus and weight change. At times, it is the center of preoccupation (i.e., figure); at others, it colors the background (i.e., ground). Our attempt to understand this kind of life involved an ongoing movement between viewing violence as figure or ground. Thus, in some cases, violence is the focus of inquiry; in others, it become the lens through which the couplehood is examined. Some of the chapters look at the violence itself. Violence is the figure, the outcome variable. Our goal in such chapters was to understand what affects violence, how it evolves. In other chapters, we focused on violence as ground. Here, violence became the explanatory variable, and we attempt to understand its impact on relationships and on the perceptions, understandings, and behaviors of protagonists involved in it. The shifting salience of violence in the various chapters reflects its interchangeably marginal or central location in the partners' joint life.

The unit of analysis for the book is the couple. However, this should not be understood in the sense that we were looking for one voice of the couple as a unit or that we attempted to merge their experiences. On the contrary, we examined the interactions among individuals who are separate in their meaning systems, intentions, perceptions, relative inputs, and responsibility for the violent events. By simultaneously examining the violent men's and battered women's interpretations of violence, and by showing the dialectic nature of these interpretations, we hope to shed light on what perpetuates the men's abusive behavior and continuous power over the women and the causes that keep women connected to their violent partners. In addition, our choice of the couple as the unit of analysis is related to the fact that many of our interviewees and clients over the years referred to themselves as *self-in-couple*. Both survivors and perpetrators continued viewing themselves as couples in spite of their awareness of the negative social definitions applied to them, mostly by professionals who placed them in deviant roles. Given this, couplehood should be viewed as an essential contextual variable for understanding the individual experiences of our informants. Our guiding criteria in choosing the couple or the men and women as separate groups as the focus of our analysis were the need to remain faithful to informants' experiences and to avoid fragmenting the data in a way that distorted their meaning. For example, in the chapter examining metaphors, we treated men and women as two separate groups, because they seldom used similar metaphors or referred to their partners' metaphors. On the other hand, the development of the violent event was perceived as interactive and couple based. This does not mean that the inputs of the partners in the emergence of or the responsibility for the violence were equal. Neither should it be understood as providing justification for the man's violence against his partner. However, we believe that any attempt to present the woman as a passive nonparticipant in the escalation process works as a boomerang that is likely to lead to victim blaming. It goes without saying that the woman may stand up for herself, may struggle, resist, and attempt to break taken-for-granted understandings based on gender. By ignoring her as an agent, we imply that her input needs to be masked, which in turn leads to the implicit position that certain behavioral inputs from her side call for violence from his side. This way, we convey the message that violence in such cases may be justified and even deserved.

The data from the interviews throughout the book were analyzed from a phenomenological perspective, which maintains that reality needs to be understood as people experience it in their consciousness (e.g., Schutz, 1967). Thus, we were interested in understanding intimate violence in the everyday world of those who live it, from their own viewpoints. However, we do not maintain, as the phenomenologists do, that a synthesis of individual meanings will lead to an understanding of the invariant structure or the essence of the phenomenon under scrutiny. Rather, we believe that constructed realities reflected by those individual meanings are pluralistic and relativistic. They are socially and culturally bound and need to be contextualized in time, place, history, and language. In other words, intimate violence cannot be understood apart from the characteristics of the couples' social and cultural milieu, such as lifestyles, beliefs and attitudes concerning right and wrong, legitimization of violence, norms related to the woman's place in various social units, and laws regulating social behavior. Behavior patterns, just like meaning systems, are also context bound. A major insight related to behavior patterns gained through this study highlights the severe limitations on the choices people make. Most of our informants seemed to be under a powerful, dynamic force that engulfed them like a whirlwind and in the thrall of rituals whose beginnings dictate their ends, according to prereflective, predetermined scripts. This mesmerizing power of habits and patterns weakens free choice as it makes it context dependent.

To fully explore this conclusion, and to explain the powerful impact of context on behavior patterns, we have used some concepts from social constructivism (Gergen, 1994). In the remainder of this chapter, we present the major ideas of constructivist thinking, and we point out how these figure throughout the book.

Constructivism maintains that people construct the reality in which they live. They interpret and make sense of their lives through the invention of abstract structures, organized into concepts, which are used to understand the world. Social constructivism focuses on the creation of collective meaning. The concepts used for understanding the world and ourselves are shaped by linguistic and communicative conventions through interpersonal interaction, negotiation, and social exchange (Lincoln & Guba, 1985; Potter, 1996; Schwandt, 1994). Thus, the construction of reality cannot be understood outside the social and cultural context in which it is created. One major implication of constructivist thinking is that events, experiences, situations, and phenomena are susceptible to many different constructions. Because these constructions are rooted in specific sociocultural contexts, any "truth" will have to be taken as relative rather than absolute. What we take to be an objective truth is culturally and socially rooted.

The book presents the multiple faces of the constructed realities among cohabitant couples living in violence, the impact of context on the formulations of their constructions, and the changes in meaning arising from changes in context.

How can we understand people's life stories from such a perspective? Forms of storytelling exist within a society and guide individual stories people tell about themselves. The acquisition of the skills required for the use of cultural narratives occurs through interaction with others. In the process, people create a collective index. Their stories reflect the social expectations regarding the telling of a "good story." People experience themselves and others in terms of socially imposed structures of story lines, such as beginnings, low points, climaxes, and endings. A number of widely known functional narratives used for a variety of purposes can be identified. For instance, one can provide an account for violence that encapsulates a narrative of stability when one needs to present a well-established self or another one that includes a progressive narrative when change is called for and valued.

Just as people are channeled into given story lines, they are directed into sequences of activities and rituals, which are determined by cultural scripts. The idea that people are limited in their free choice, that they are conditioned by social rituals to walk down a limited number of preimposed paths, is deeply rooted in the constructivist tradition. According to Gergen (1994), hostility that escalates to violence is an example of such a script: the anatomy of foreknown violence! The development of an emotionally charged event, such as hostility, proceeds according to a set of rules. These rules draw their vitality and effectiveness from culturally derived standards. The participants are like protagonists in a social dance that consists of well known and coordinated steps and that evolves according to established rules, norms, and stable patterns. Hence, interpersonal hostilities should not be perceived as external expressions of inner feelings but as forms of cultural performance.

From such a perspective, intimate violence is an example of a relationship pattern that takes an undesirable path. But once the script is initiated, both partners have little choice but to continue walking along the path prescribed by it. When partners are trapped in a scenario where the beginning signals its end, the violence may be experienced as appropriate and even desirable to one or both of them. The theme of social scripts is one of the building blocks in this book. Chapter 2 illustrates the steps of the social dance that partners living in violence perform while sliding from isolated violent events to a violent way of life. It presents the dynamics of swirling and sinking into violent rituals. Chapter 3 analyzes the behavior patterns following violent events and identifies the stages of the recovery rituals that are meant to preserve couplehood and allow the formulation of understandings for continuous shared life. Chapter 4 examines the daily routine of partners living in violence and analyzes the cyclical movement from order to disorder and back to a renewed order. It also presents the gap between the rigidity of the script, which serves as an anchor for everyday life, and the fragility of joint life that is subject to the script. Chapter 5 describes the process by which love, guilt, and violence are all fused together. From a situation where love, guilt, and violence are experienced as disparate and contradictory, we move to one in which they become a single emotion. Chapter 6 analyzes the meanings reflected in the metaphors used by men and women living in violence. These metaphors have the power of reducing the partners' courses of action to the point of entrapping them in scenarios that limit their choices of behavior. Chapter 7 presents accounts of the violence given by partners and demonstrates the socially available story lines for interpreting violence within a social and cultural environment that condemns it. Chapter 8 describes how contradictory scripts held respectively by law enforcement agents and partners affect the power balance in the family in a manner that may contribute to an exacerbation of the violence. Chapter 9 expounds the guidelines for intervention while heuristically applying the various theoretical concepts presented throughout the book.

Intimate violence can be envisioned as urban warfare in which a single incident has flared up into an all-out, self-fueled confrontation. It is a war that is not planned by generals; its moves are unanticipated and no retreat lines are marked. Yet something directs it: It unfolds according to a social script, which becomes a trap. The trap tightens its grip in various situations by diverse means, via language, emotions, behavior, in everyday life, during and after violent events, reflectively and prereflectively. It engulfs the partners through a predictable ritual, constructing a way of life out of a single occurrence of violence. Following violent events, efforts are made to reach joint understandings. Although at first glance these may seem to be escape routes, given their being based on conflicting expectations, they lead to deadlock. The aftermath of violence is a temporary cease-fire, a time to lick the wounds, to cash in on tentative advantages, to recover, and to gather strength for the next round. Violence is woven into the process and occasionally rears its face. It is pregnant with the seeds of renewed escalation. The grip is further tightened in everyday life, which is conducted within a rigid, hierarchical organization, emphasizing clear role division and territories. The rigidity of the frame, which leaves no room for dialogue, is easily cracked, allowing the "we-ness" to escape. Truth is replaced by falsehood, we-ness by alienation. Two separate and parallel realities establish themselves. Violence becomes a way of controlling threatening differences. The grip is tightened through a language rich in metaphors of war, which serve to preserve the reality of being in combat. Capitulation, risk, retaliation, fear and threat, defense and survival, control and loss are but a few examples. Language also marks the escape routes: Denials, settling of accounts, and the like, are all meant to persuade the self and the other that the war must continue. Emotion tightens the grip. In the complex emotional dynamics in which love and hate intermingle, love paradoxically becomes a catalyst of violence. Doubts about its existence, the fear of losing it, the will to conquer it, all these contribute to reconstructing violence as an expression of love and to construing war as a standardized means of negotiating responsibility and guilt. The trap closes with the appearance of control agents in the couple's lives. Once they fail to break the circle of hostility through dialogue, those who were expected to be the saviors become instruments in fortifying the trenches, part of the arsenal, enlisted in the campaign against the opposite camp.

Intimate violence, then, goes beyond raising a hand. It is present when the partners withdraw to refresh their strength, to negotiate a cease-fire, to live their everyday lives, to account for their behavior, to interpret the perspective of the other, and to reconstruct the reality of their lives through plausible narratives. One must understand intimate violence as rooted in a complex and multidimensional context that contributes to it and is shaped by it. The context changes according to the dynamics of the relationship, and it constitutes the relationship's volatile foundation. The constant changes in the definition of boundaries, trust, values and priorities, interpretations of the other, achievements and compromises, victories and defeats, the sense of power and control, and responsibility all make up the ever-fluctuating context that brings about the reenactment of the violent scene.

Western societies are socially and culturally heterogeneous. They include subcultures with diverse values, priorities, and moral and ethical rules. People are socialized into the broader, dominant culture as well as into the specific subculture in which they live, as if they were living in a bilingual society. In the passage from the broader culture to a subculture, or vice versa, the rules of the game change. The meanings of what is true and false, permitted or forbidden, vary according to the cultural scene. For instance, the perception of the other, the woman, or the children as possessions is part of a specific subcultural perception. In other words, the ontological agreements concerning reality are embedded in the social framework in which members claim membership. In a world of multiple realities that imposes divergent criteria for truth, and in which we hold simultaneous membership in several frameworks, the attempt to build couplehood based on rigid principles is doomed to failure. Among such divergent realities and understandings, where diverse cultural voices emerge as alternatives, the questioning of the rigid boundaries of the couplehood is to be expected. Such rigid tendencies are expressed by power- and control-based constructions, subordinate-superordinate relationships, sharp territorial divisions, perceptions of woman as property, and a constant questioning of traditional role definitions. The rigidity paralyzes the dialogue and makes negotiation and partnership difficult if not impossible. But it cannot arrest the tempestuous undercurrents. Violence becomes a desperate attempt to hold on to the principles of the subculture in an uphill battle.

When the earth shakes, we see attempts to handle experiences of loss or of potential loss: threats to the hierarchy, invasion of territory, loss of love, loss of victory, the threat of paying the social price. The threat is pervasive and includes everything considered "mine," everything a person owns, his manhood, her womanhood, the roles defining their identity, everything. Violence as the sole recourse in the struggle cannot retrieve the loss, and thus its very use generates the next loss. Hence, within the system of rituals and scripts that led to it, there is no option of abandoning it, and it is never beneficial. It is a no-win game. Perhaps the legend of the Dutch boy can illustrate the violent man's predicament. The boy tries to block the leaks in the dam with his finger to prevent his country from being flooded, but he cannot keep up with the leaks, having used all his fingers. Hence, a great flood is about to take place. This is the anatomy of the foreknown flood. Violence is a desperate attempt to block more and more leaks in the dam. It is a strategy that attempts to avoid the dyadic hell by creating it.

From a constructivist point of view, intimate violence should be seen as a socially constructed emotional expression anchored in a set of cultural rules. Within these cultural dicta, inequality among men and women is an essential component. This book focuses on the personal and interpersonal experience of intimate violence from the participants' viewpoint, and thus allocates little space for analyzing the social and historical roots that shaped its emergence. However, personal experiences of intimate violence should always be located, understood, and interpreted in the light of sociohistorical facts, such as unequal power distribution, differential rights, cultural norms based on discrimination, status discrepancies, and unequal access to resources. While reading this book, the reader would do well to keep the aforementioned context always in view. A perception of intimate violence as socially constructed implies that the path leading to violence is one possible course among several others. Violence is not the only possible outcome of scripts of hostility and anger in gender relations. Thus, within the dialectic between individuals and social scripts, choices are still to be made. The raised hand is not society's but the individual man's, his choice and responsibility. Yet it does have social connotations in that it reflects the culturally accepted arrangements that govern gender relations. At the heart of the constructivist approach is the urge to bring out as many alternative scripts as possible and emphasize rather than blur the issue of individual choice and responsibility.

As has been mentioned, throughout the book, we have used a phenomenological perspective to analyze the interviews and a constructivist conceptual scheme to establish them in their broader social and cultural settings. The former proved to be useful in understanding the meaning of intimate violence on the personal and interpersonal levels and allowed for a conceptualization based on multiple voices. The latter provided the tools for understanding the power of society in shaping the meanings described. Once we unveil the existence of social scripts and related social dicta, we will be able to consider change. We may reexamine what has been previously considered as assumed truth and thus, to some measure, liberate our thought and behavioral patterns from the enormous social forces limiting them.

2

The Violent Event

From Violent Incidents to Violent Rituals

Attempting to understand violent events is a complicated and tricky business for the researcher and the clinician, as well as for the actual participants. In our research, no less than in our clinical work, we found that such attempts were met with resistance on the part of those participants who systematically suppressed all evaded memory of the violence because of emotional and cognitive difficulties. Survivors and perpetrators are faced with a seemingly contradictory task. On the one hand, violence presents them with a distorted and ugly image of themselves and their partners, which they feel a need to reject. On the other hand, violence induces a need to understand it, to reflect on its meaning, as a precondition for being able to continue living with oneself and with one's partner. Our interviewees were living under the pressure of these two opposing forces. Whereas some described the event as if it "hit them," others presented us with a well-processed and reinterpreted understanding of the event, after subjecting it to systematic scrutiny and reflection. At times, both men and women declared that they did not understand what happened, but on reflection, they said that at the time, they found themselves in a situation of violence in which they felt as nonparticipants. The event was strangely incoherent and discontinuous with respect to all other events in their life. They were unable to account for the event to themselves and therefore incapable of communicating it. For other interviewees, the violence was clear and goal oriented. They felt that violence was instrumental in achieving an aim that could not be achieved otherwise.

Some survivors take the violence for granted as part of their lives; therefore, there is nothing striking enough about it to warrant reflection or attention. Others experience the violence as shocking, horrible, and life threatening. Terror surrounds them, so they are constantly on the alert and constantly prepared in anticipation of its recurrence.

As for the perpetrators, their acts of violence threaten their self-respect and attack the core of their basic "decency." They consequently tend to view it as disfiguring their true natures. Hence, they attempt to avoid analyzing or clarifying the violent event. From their standpoints, the violence is often called for and therefore rational. It is a problem-solving tool that they regard as beneficial not only to them but to the victim and the entire family. It is mostly perceived as occurring for the last time, if the victim would only understand what to do to avoid it. The men believe they know what should be done differently to avoid it in the future but that it is up to the women to change. Because many women share this philosophy, it becomes integral to their joint belief system. Some partners attempted to regulate the memories of violent events as time went by so as to engineer a psychological distance from them sufficient for maintaining a bearable joint framework.

It must be borne in mind that in this book the discussion of the development of violent events concerns partners who remained together in spite of the violence. There is an inherent contradiction in these violent events: On the one hand, such events are extremely distressing and harmful for the dyadic relationship; on the other, they often become a means of communication, interaction, and an arena of resolving pending issues. Thus, the violent event should be understood as a puzzle that is composed of immediate and situational factors as well as a variety of diachronic historical ones. Our analysis will draw on the phenomenological understanding of the consciousness involved and on the emerging meanings that compose the puzzle—the event as it is "given" to us.

The experience of violence by the interviewees was not homogeneous. However, there was a continuum of living with violence, ranging from experiencing it as an incident, an isolated occurrence, to making it part of everyday life and developing a relatively high degree of tolerance for it. Several thematic junctions were identified along this continuum. One was violence as related to specific topics; the other was violence as related to lack of trust; a third was violence for the sake of one individual at the expense of his significant other; the fourth was the engulfment in violence as a way of life. These themes were intermeshed and could be found in most accounts of violent events. But as time went on, a process transpired whereby specific events were translated into lack of trust, which in turn led to self-centered attitudes, separateness, and last, to a high tolerance of violence as part of dyadic life.

Violence Related to Specific Topics

Most couples have experiential knowledge as to which of their rows is likely to become a violent event. Although they often have a recollection of the details of what they were arguing about, they usually fail to fix these in a context that can give them a broader perspective and enable them to understand the ways in which the violent events evolved and became part of their lives. This is particularly so concerning the issue of gender relations. Although they do have a superficial understanding of the multiple ways in which gender affects the power relations between them, men seldom make this connection explicit in spite of women's attempts to bring their experience of power and gender to the forefront.

Three dominant topics were identified in our research around which violent events of this kind develop: conflicts about money and economic concerns (which were usually related), arguments about the division of household duties and chores, and conflicts concerning the children. The couple quoted here quarreled mostly about the division of chores and about money.

One woman said,

> I don't get angry easily. Things can happen and I don't care. But there are other things, which tick me off. The house, the education of the kids, the jobs around the house . . . you do the bathing of the kids, do the laundry, lots about the money. Above all, I am not allowed to spend a penny.

Her male partner said,

> I told her: "Why would you want to come with me. You need to take care of the house." She told me, "What do you care, the house will be taken care of." She turned around and went out for a walk. I came home and I saw she brought in a housekeeper. I told her, "You don't

work, I am the only breadwinner". . . . I hate it when I am being lied
to. For me, this is like betrayal. If a person is capable of lying, he is
capable of doing anything. That's how the violence between us
started.

In a different context, the same woman stated in the interview, "I
always hide ten shekels. If I need it for the hairdresser . . . or something. He knows about every shekel he spends on himself but doesn't
always tell me." These quotes show the partners' divergent interpretations of common issues. The man considers himself the sole breadwinner, and as such, he is entitled to control the woman's space and
actions. He clearly presents these expectations to the woman. The
woman, on the other hand, feels that there is no division of labor, no
partnership, and that she is being used and controlled. She identifies
those aspects in the argument that are unbearable to her and that will
place her in the position of being forced to react. The man feels it is
not his duty to control his actions but rather to achieve a division of
labor that is just, to which the woman must conform. If she doesn't,
she is in obvious breach of contract from his perspective. Once she
does not live up to her responsibility, he feels betrayed and thus entitled to react violently. The woman feels that in such an over-
controlling situation, she needs the small lies to survive and considers
those as legitimate. The man knows she is lying and thus sees himself
entitled to tighten his control. This creates a general atmosphere of
distrust and suspicion so that specific lies lose their acuteness.

Another key issue that induces conflict is the children. The analysis of the interviews shows that the woman views children as a central
vital concern in themselves. The man in his turn perceives her preoccupation with them and her claim for control over this domain as an
additional means to assert her power and to exclude him. This in turn
is interpreted by many men as humiliation. The perspectives of the
two partners are polarized. The men are described by women as
overpunitive and without real concern for their children. Men view
the women's behavior as part of a power struggle with them. The
women claim the issues related to the children as their exclusive province from which the man is kept out. Such attitudes are perceived by
men as preventing them from expressing their "good selves" and from
developing relationships with their children. Overall, the man interprets the process as loss and introduces violence as a means to regain
what he perceives as loss of power, exclusion, and a direct attack on
his family status. One woman said,

He does not know how to punish the children appropriately. He can
be too tough with his punishments even though they didn't do much.

We have lots of disagreements over this. He tells me, "Don't mess in this." I can't stay out of it. It makes me upset he is doing that to my children, not only his.

The man, on the other hand, stated,

The conflicts were around the issue of me being consistent in my approach to education. If I promise something, I try to deliver most of the time. For better or worse, I stood behind my word, while Nurith (a pseudonym) wavers constantly. She would scream that I am not acting right. It boils down to the fact that I am always wrong with the children.

Or another woman:

I keep telling him I prefer to stay with the children. So he would start getting upset and scream. I prefer the children over him. He hits me when I tell him, "What about this stuff I told you to buy, the eyeglasses for the kid."

Her partner said,

Most of the time, we argue over the children. She consults with me but then does what she thinks is good for them. And then we argue. Most of the time, we argue with the children present. I can tell they are wondering. . . . You can tell they don't like it at all. I get really upset and am trying not to blow up . . . and hit her.

It seems obvious from the foregoing quotes that the territorial power struggles between the partners are related to their general ideas as to the allocation of domains of authority according to gender and not merely to local conflicts about their own children. One side is attempting to perpetuate his or her control over a certain area, whereas the other is trying to invade it. One's partner's actual control is viewed as a deliberate violation of one's individual rights. In this kind of conflict, there is an ongoing conflating of role and personality in which the man usually perceives himself as authorized to enforce an equitable "social contract" whose validity is self-evident to him. When this authority of his is challenged, the ensuing power struggles engender loss of trust and constant suspicion.

At some point, the deeper motive for violence (e.g., distrust) is dissociated from its immediate specific reasons (e.g., an unfair division of chores and responsibilities, or lies). The violence becomes part of a symbolic cycle, which is self-contained and self-perpetuating. The woman is always suspect, the man on alert, and he needs an occasion to administer a preemptive blow to keep his partner in her place. In this context, his violence is not part of a specific sequence of causes and effects but rather a reasonable option, as he sees it. Such a view is supported by the overall social context of unequal gender relations that serves as support for the man's attitude and behaviors, but he seldom reflects on it.

Violence as Related to the Loss of Trust

In the previous section, violence was seen as event related. Here, we shall observe the way it extends beyond specific occurrences, forcibly coloring the entire relationship. The experience accumulated by the partners in violence generates distrust that underlines all future interactions. The loss of trust becomes the dominant affective mode of the relationship. Violence is not necessarily justified by the perpetrator on the basis of actual occurrences (e.g., she was spending unreasonably and the hitting was meant to bring her to reason), it is now justified by anticipation (e.g., she gets beaten because she cannot keep from spending). Originally, violence was conceived as a means for changing situations. Now, it has become a means of altering relationships. One woman said,

> In the beginning, I was spending a lot of money and he didn't know. I got into many debts. I was afraid to tell him about the debts because he would get mad, leave his job, and give up. . . . It was sort of a mixed-up situation. When he found out, he lost trust in me. Now, whatever I do, he doesn't believe me . . . and in everything he does, I don't believe him. And there is a wall between us.

The man said,

> I come home and she starts screaming. I ask, "Where is the money?" She tells me she paid, I tell her "I checked it out and you did not." She doesn't tell me where the money went. She digs in and I get more heated up. She never says anything about where the money is and I keep heating up.

Efforts are made by the parties to settle old accounts between them while they are trying to restore trust and faith. In fact, these attempts are the basis for further conflict, arguments, and continuing lack of trust. The man's attempt to find out what happened is governed by a preexisting scenario, which tends to lead toward more conflict. For the woman the wall of distrust leads to silence. There is no point in attempting to communicate. The silence of the woman is construed by the man as a sign of recognition of her guilt, and it justifies his regarding her as unreliable. The woman perceives the couple as trapped together in a situation of loss of trust, whereas the man regards himself and his partner as two separate individuals in adverse positions. Thus, the man interprets the conflictual situation as aggression directed toward him personally. Another man expressed this as follows:

Pnina, instead of talking with me and telling me what is bothering her, she would simply go and buy a nice dress, and buy things for the children. And the money was gone. . . . She would vent her anger by spending money. . . . Instead of talking to me, she would spend money. . . . She wanted to hurt me by this. She could not hurt me any other way. I feel she is guilty. . . . I hold her responsible for the whole thing with my anger.

His partner said,

The entire responsibility of taking care of the house and the children was on me. . . . I had no one to share it with. And it was hard. He wasn't involved in any of this stuff. He never knew that things are as difficult as they were. . . . I didn't want to involve him. I thought I could handle it myself. I saw I couldn't. So it got to him. All the money issues. He found out and he was angry at me. I was feeling that it hurt him at some point, but on the other hand, he didn't do anything. He never asked, What did you buy? What do we have? What do we need? When he's arguing, he gets angry, and I used to react by being afraid to talk to him about these topics.

The man assumes that the woman's silence is a sign that "everything is in order." The woman is silent because she knows from past experience that any attempt to communicate problems will only lead to more anger and resistance. Her fear to speak out and her subsequent silence is now reinterpreted by the man as an acknowledgment of guilt and hostile unwillingness to involve him in her struggle. When the man finds out that problems were hidden, he sees her reticence as "lies" and as intended to humiliate him. He attempts to reestablish control by further escalating his anger by violence. This in turn confirms the woman in her conviction that she was right to keep silent. The man often interpreted her silence as aggressive:

I keep screaming and at times I slap her. After the slap, the argument is over because she starts crying. . . . If she cries, the argument ends.

> When a person cries, she usually is sorry for what she does. If she does not cry and I see that her answer does not satisfy me, I keep arguing. I keep it up until she levels with me on this and cries.

The woman responds to his attempts to dominate by shutting down:

> I'd rather not answer in such situations. I prefer to shut up. But this creates more arguments. He constantly goes back to the same issues. It makes me angry and I prefer not to talk about it. I know if I talk, it's arguments again. . . . So I've had it. I prefer to shut up. I became indifferent. I don't answer and I don't talk.

The man interprets the woman's crying and her pain as a confession. Her crying is a sign that he has finally reached rock bottom with her—and that the truth is his truth. He assumes her guilt, and therefore, her crying must be a mere mask for her guilt rather than a genuine expression of pain. The man feels that by losing trust in his partner, his inner peace has been shattered; he blames her, and he feels justified in keeping the woman in fear to deprive her of her inner peace in return. As for the woman, whether she talks or keeps silent, she will always achieve the same results. When she chooses disengagement as a means of survival or safety, the man regards her as dodging her guilt and exhibiting the intention to continue arguing.

Loss of trust leads to further loss of trust. Violence is used on the assumption that trust can be restored. When this expectation is thwarted, the lack of trust receives further reinforcement in the relationship. These spiral processes lead to gradual separation; we-ness vanishes, and violence is used to advance selfish goals. The couple dissolves into two self-centered individuals.

Using Violence to Foster Individual Goals

At this point, there is a shift from mutual to individual goals, with the realization that fulfilling one's goals will necessarily be at the expense of the other.

Men view themselves as entitled to set the norms of interpreting their partners' behaviors. They expect their partners to be predictable and nonthreatening. When women argue back, their taken-for-granted submissiveness is lost, and men experience this as a threat. The woman is perceived as undergoing total transformation. A man said,

She has a heart of gold. She is shy. If she's OK, there is no problem and all is quiet, in its place. But when she starts arguing, she becomes a whole different person. She becomes stubborn. She changes from cover to cover.

His partner said,

I discovered many things alone, things that he was hiding. And I get angry. And I start asking questions. We raise our voices, and I am about to break down and shout. The same mechanical answers, full of lies. This is what makes me the angriest.

The man quoted here attempted to present his wife as cantankerous and as undergoing some incomprehensible personality change—from being quiet and docile to being quarrelsome. Thus, he perceives her as responsible for changing the interpersonal atmosphere and for provoking the arguments. The woman, for her part, sees the bickering and the confrontations as the only recourse for circumventing what she calls his lies. It is her only rational way to change the content of the argument. In this process, the argument is gradually detached from its original content, and it becomes a power struggle, each partner trying to impose his or her view on the other. The man distinguishes between the woman who was "shy" (in other words, had no goals of her own and was fulfilling his expectations) and the one who is "stubborn" (focused on her own goals at her partner's expense). Such a total transformation is temporary here and signals the shift from shared goals to individual, conflicting goals. This pattern may stabilize over time and become the governing modus operandi of the couple. Under these circumstances, violent action is resorted to, not only to redirect her to mutual goals but also to protect his own. The woman also feels alone, now that she finds herself needing to protect her own interests against his so-called lies. Her loneliness is a reaction to the man's self-serving behavior, keeping to himself and his own interests. Her questioning is aimed at discovering his true self, which he has been hiding from her. The questioning leads to violence, which paradoxically preserves the union because it prevents the revelation that they have little in common. The same man further stated, regarding the violence,

She thinks she is the one in this house who makes the decisions. She decides what will be done, and I have no say in it. She thinks she's right and not even God can make her change her mind. . . . She'll continue with the argument, even if she gets beaten she doesn't care. What counts is that she's right. . . . I hit her to deter her. To stop her and make an end to it. You wouldn't stop it, you'll get more of the same.

The woman said,

I didn't expect to be hit. He doesn't usually do things like this. It takes a long time to get him upset because he's usually indifferent. But what I have to say, I will, and we'll keep arguing forever.

In the previous quotes, what was illustrated was the nature of the relationship. Here, partners are seen as explaining the nature of the violence and its rationale. As far as the man is concerned, violence is used for deterrence purposes. The woman reads it as a sign of not being indifferent. The bottom line is that both partners view violence as a means of continuing their relationship, without expecting the violence to solve anything. The woman expects them to argue forever and the man expects the so-called argument to continue. The man attempts to reestablish control through violence, the woman attempts to resist it. Violence can accommodate both of these positions. Paradoxically, violence remains the only common ground left for the partners to dig into and foster each their separate agendas. However, partners are not likely to recognize this, and they need other frameworks for continuing their shared life. One such frame that we identified was the perception of arguments as a struggle between competing principles. The struggle becomes a fight for the endurance of one's autonomous self, and surrender is associated with a sense of severe loss in terms of selfhood to the adversary. As one man said,

One can give in only up to a certain point. A man has his own ideas, and he cannot give in on those. There are principles that one cannot give up even at the expense of arguments and quarrels. A man cannot lose his personality. Otherwise, he is a nobody. To avoid arguments, he needs to shut up here and there. What has such a man done? He made himself into someone else, and I don't intend to make myself into someone else, even if I need to argue.

The woman said,

I am explaining the things the way I would want him to behave. He's not willing to listen. He always thinks he's right. There is no way to dispute it with him. There is a phase in which I can avoid arguments. But there are things that I cannot put up with, so I can't shut up. I argue, I am capable of raising my voice when I see he's not right.

I don't think he listens, but he knows he's making a mistake. But he would never recognize he's wrong.

Common to these partners is that they perceive the argument as a struggle for truth and justice. This does not preclude the power dimension related to control and submission. However, this is done in a personalized moral framework. They both tacitly draw some imaginary limit beyond which they will not move and cannot compromise. They both consider escalation as legitimate when the conflict exceeds this limit. The man experiences the failure to respect these boundaries as deliberately directed against him. The woman is trying to convince the man that he is wrong, knowing he thinks he's always right. The vicious circle is inevitable. To the man, the argument is also futile, for he believes he must not give in, because every compromise will bring him closer to the point of threat to his selfhood. There is no real dialogue then, only monologues that are bound to escalate.

As the escalation unfolds, the man and the woman become firm in their convictions that the other one is vicious and merely taking advantage of their weakness. They both feel inferior and vulnerable. Two interrelated structural features characterize the violent conflict at this point. One is of a moral or doctrinal nature, the other tactical.

On the moral plane, giving in to the other for the sake of reaching some compromise is conceived as tantamount to self-betrayal. It is a sheer violation of authenticity, of being true to oneself. The existential choice, then, is to be or not to be true to oneself. Now, because in the kind of situation we are dealing with, the question of dissolving the couplehood does not even arise; maintaining one's integrity can only be achieved within the relationship. Action in the most drastic sense is called for, and in this light, beating one's wife doesn't seem an unreasonable price to pay. Strikingly enough, this boldly consequential line of reasoning stops short of recognizing the opposition's right to salvage *her* integrity. The underlying assumption might well be that the protagonist is not quite sure that she really has a truth of her own. The very acknowledgment, at any rate, that the other deserves consideration of any kind casts doubt on the purity of one's moral position. And if one is not morally superior, one tends to feel inferior and vulnerable.

One woman said,

Whenever I try to talk to him and attempt to come to a compromise, he behaves as if he knows he can do to me anything he feels like. He laughs at me, makes me look like a fool. And I am a person who gives

everything, to all people and from a position of equality, even if he is
as bad as he was this time. First, I assume you're good. He knows
that, and he uses me.

At the same time, the man said,

Even if I come home at 11 at night, if I know my wife worked the
same day, that would be enough for me. I would clean the house at
night and would help her to do the dishes. And there is no time limit.
But when you feel that you do everything all the time and get no
appreciation, you stop doing it. You just get desperate.

The partners mirror each other's feelings that being good is a weakness. They gradually develop a strong sense that they must always be
on the alert because the other's main goal is to abuse them. They
weigh every joint undertaking in terms of pain given or taken. The
other is suspect, and the man's abusive behavior is seen as inherent in
his personality. A man said, "I told her, Look . . . you refuse to see . . .
whatever I do for you. You first always try to find what is wrong with
what I did. And that's the problem." She said, "I am nothing to him."
The woman also describes her partner, using character terminology:

He keeps demanding and demanding but doesn't know how to
give. . . He is getting himself jacked up to get upset. . . . He's impulsive and can hit me. But that's the only way he knows. He is coward.
He is constantly afraid.

Because the woman regards her partner as a coward, she believes
that verbal abuse will set limits for him, and she uses it: "If he is with
me and he says something I don't like . . . he'll be careful, he knows
that I will be all over him." The man, on the other hand, said: "I'll hit
her. Let's say I slap her. If she wants to protect herself she'll go to the
other room and it'll be all over. But if she doesn't do that, she'll hit
back, she'll throw things, she'll scream." The woman said: "When it
starts, I'll push him. Sometimes, I can hit him too. And I'd tell him, You
don't enjoy it, ha? You want to continue? Then let's continue." The
man described the way he sees the logic of the same situation:

When a woman hits and she allows herself to swear, there must be a
limit. . . . In the middle of the argument, you get to a point where you
keep talking and you see the other person respond with his hands.
You get to the point that you realize that without hands it wouldn't
work. You use her method.

The previous quotes show an escalatory process in which each partner adheres to his or her private logic in understanding the events and is caught up in this logic to the utter inability to see that the other also has a perspective, a subjectivity. To convince the other, they use the very same tactics that they find so objectionable when used by their partners. Their attempts then to stop violence are also violent. The woman hopes to stop the man from hurting her by inflicting pain on him so he can experience it. She is trying to make him feel what she feels. The man needs to stop her from behaving like a man, and this can only be done by using a man's force. The woman feels that the man is aggressive but out of weakness and fear. She is afraid of him, yet she also believes that setting boundaries by the use of violence is effective. When she swears or hits back, her behavior is felt by him to be utterly unbefitting a woman (not sufficiently distinguished from his manhood). This in turn warrants his further reaction and justifies his violence. From his perspective, fleeing would have been both more appropriate and more feminine and would possibly have ended the violence.

We have attempted to show so far how members of couples living in violence become self-centered individuals denying the other and transforming him or her into an object. Violence remains the only common ground that sustains the relationship, both the reason and the outcome of their remaining together. If up to this point it was possible somehow to distinguish between the relationship itself and the violent incident occurring within it, now they have become one: The relationship *is* violence.

Violence as a Way of Life

Once the violence and the relationship become synonymous, they cannot be separated. The man, the woman, and the violence are fused together. Whereas previously, violence was either the consequence or the cause of specific situations, now it has turned into a personality trait. As one man said,

> On one hand, she tells me this story about fear. On the other hand, I know she knows well that if we were to take account over the whole time period, over all these years we have been arguing, I never really hurt her or the children seriously. The worst it came to was a slap. . . . Nurith wants me to change my truth, that I won't be so real, that I won't be so sincere. And I can't do it. It is against my character.

Because self-denial is now recognized as impossible, being true to his own character is the only morally feasible possibility. Although violence is established as the only course, it needs now to be presented as the *right* way. To do this, the violent man needs to socially justify his violence. Thus, he cannot afford to see his partner as "just frightened"; he needs to attribute resiliency and power to her and enough influence over his life to make his violence plausible. He goes on to indicate that he can be violent and also in control of his violence, as opposed to the woman who is presented as uncontrolled and unpredictable in *her* violence. By the use of such subliminal tactics, the man reinstates himself in a positive light, which he would have preferred his partner to reflect on him. In spite of descriptive differences, the woman views the situation quite similarly:

> I fear his attacks. I don't enjoy getting hit by cups and dishes, or his screaming. So I would just keep my mouth shut. Sometimes, I know it could end bad . . . real bad. But I would let him know in the middle of the argument that he should not do it. It doesn't help. And then he tries to tell me, "Try to stop it before it comes." It's hard, real hard. Even if I leave the room, I keep hearing him. I am afraid of him. There were times I was really afraid of him because he was threatening to kill me. At times, I believe he is capable of doing it because he has no control.

The woman accuses her partner of having characteristics similar to those he finds in her. She has a clear sense of the imminence of a thrashing but still goes through the motions of trying to forestall it. These attempts are included mainly to establish a positive social identity while presenting the partner as having lost control and as dangerous. One cannot help but see the ritualistic aspects of these symmetrical tactics. The ritual substitutes for the we-ness and binds them together in a relationship of mutual dependency. Except, they don't depend on each other as persons but on the continual joint ritual itself. Another man said,

> She would swear at me, and I would get real pissed and I would hit her. . . . I would slap her once, twice. If she couldn't stop swearing, I would slap her. I would feel this is not a solution, but I guess I haven't found a better one. I had no solution other than this situation. I am not a person who gets angry easily. I am calm. I like it when there are no problems. Everything is smooth. But it was a situation I couldn't take any longer.

The woman partner said,

> When we would have arguments, there would be a lot of verbal vio-
> lence on my side and physical violence on his. We complemented
> each other. . . . I would swear and scream, and he wasn't ready to
> hear. The minute he raises his hands, I try to get back at him. He did
> bad stuff to you, you do it back to him. I don't want to owe him.
> That's how I feel: You'll get it yourself and you'll feel it. But he's
> stronger, so I would get more.

The main characteristic of rituals is that the participants act in them
according to a given and familiar script defined by context. The occurrences are predictable, step by step: There will be name calling and
screaming by the woman, experienced and equated by the man with
his physical violence. He further views her verbal abuse as fueling his
physical one and the other way around. When the context is a violent
way of life, the woman views her name calling as aggression, directed
to get back at him. This creates an endless, vicious circle in the perception of both partners. The couple bases the perpetuation of violence
on mutual needs. Though the violence is predictable, as previously
described, the woman's reaction here is based on her need to achieve
equality in the use of violent force. This ensures that the motion in a
circle will be perpetual. The vicious circle is further exacerbated by the
fact that each partner interprets the other's behavior as provocative:
The woman screams, the man refuses to hear, the woman screams
louder, the man hits her, the woman reciprocates. The woman wants
to continue screaming but also wants her partner to stop beating her.
The man similarly wants to keep slapping the woman and wants her to
stop screaming. Each is focused on controlling the other rather than
himself or herself. Once the script takes effect, violent incidents are
transformed into a violent way of life. The conversion is complete,
and the ritual of violence is their new religion. They are committed to
it, and no specific reason is needed to trigger it.

Summary

This chapter attempted to describe and analyze the ways in which
partners' experiences are dynamically framed by violent events, leading to constructed realities in which situational violence is transformed into a violent way of life. The construction process moves

through several phases, ranging from constructing violence as an isolated incident, to gradual loss of trust leading to separation and self-centeredness, and last, to becoming engulfed by violence as a way of life. During the process, the couple, as a joint enterprise, the "molecule," is broken into the two "atoms" who are essentially self-interested. They lose all trust, as well as the ability to see each other's point of view. In spite of this, the couple remains together because the ritual of violence substitutes for mutual expectations and fulfillment. Their joint reality is substituted by a polarity in which they continue living side by side. The dynamic of existing as a couple is gradually lost because any kind of dialogue is perceived as threatening, and both partners are always ready for attack or digging deeper into their defensive positions.

3

In Search of Paradise Lost

The Aftermath of Intimate Violence

The word *aftermath* is an insider's term used to delineate the time and situation immediately following violent events. Besides the chronological setting, the term refers to a qualitative modification in the experience of violence and in the expectation as to what is to follow. It further delineates at least an intermission in which the partners can begin their negotiations and reprocess their past (i.e., violent) and future (i.e., nonviolent) life. The aftermath was singled out for specific analysis because our informants invariably presented it as crucially important for understanding their experience. This may be due to the fact that when violence occurs, the expectations for a nonviolent future recede to the background; conversely, when there is no violence, these expectations advance to the forefront and violence moves to the background. The aftermath is unique in that both violence and expectations of nonviolence come to the foreground and are experienced simultaneously. Because we are addressing the experience of couples who remained together in spite of the existence of intimate violence in their lives, the aftermath can be seen as an encapsulation of their individual and joint attempts to arrive at an understanding that will keep them together. For those who may decide to part, the aftermath is likely to encapsulate the forces active in their construction of separation. Although our study deals with those couples who remained, studying the aftermath may also serve for understanding the dynamics of leaving. There is considerable disagreement between battered women and perpetrators as to when the aftermath begins and ends. Although we recognize that immediately following the violent act, there is a time of emotional and cognitive hiatus in which women are overwhelmed, numb, and detached, we do not consider this as part of the aftermath, because this stage is perceived by most women as part of the violent event.

The analysis of our interviews concerning the aftermath yielded a series of themes, which we set up into a three-stage process. First, partners analyze the damages incurred by violence; second, they attempt to renegotiate their joint life in view of the violence; and third, they attempt to actualize the newly negotiated understandings. Granted that these stages are merely schematic, they are useful in organizing the complexities involved in understanding this process.

Although men and women both viewed the aftermath as a transitional phase devoted to placing their joint life back on track, they tended to experience it differently. For instance, men tended to view the aftermath as an opportunity to achieve a deescalation and to counterbalance the violence. Their main objective was to reduce their responsibility for the violence and its general impact to manageable proportions. Women, on the other hand, tended to keep the violence and its impact as the central content of the relationship in the aftermath. In keeping with these different goals, men and women use divergent strategies to structure the aftermath. Men use strategies to pass on some of the responsibility to the partner for the events leading up to the violence, and they stress the need to confine and close the issue. Their very behavior in the aftermath subliminally serves as living proof that violence has vanished, never to return. Women, on the other hand, focus on the violence and its devastating impact. The aforementioned stages organize our analysis in this chapter.

Estimating and Controlling the Damage

Given their goals and expectations at this phase, women were understandably far more outspoken in pointing out the visibility of the damages occasioned by violence, whereas men were doing their utmost to minimize the damage. Women were dramatic, whereas men were calm; women were perceived by men as exaggerating in their descriptions of what took place, whereas men were perceived by women as trivializing the violence. For example, one woman gave a description of her experience in strong metaphoric terms:

> I felt at the time he reduced me to zero. He crushed me like a cockroach. I left to go to my sister's. My family was with me all those weeks. I wanted to die. They kept me going, helped me to raise my head and figure out where I stand with myself and my life.

Her partner considered the same incident as unworthy of all the commotion and said, "Please let's not waste time over this. It wasn't anything worth mentioning. Let's move on." The woman just quoted used metaphors of size and contrast to vividly describe her partner's success in diminishing her worth. The batterer blocks out the violence and concentrates on imposing time limitations that will greatly curtail any delving into detail. If, as he insists, what happened is so unworthy of talking about, then very little could have happened, he reasons in his mind. The woman describes the aftermath as a period in which she is deeply immersed in the pain surrounding the violent event and needs her family's support to come to terms with a life-threatening situation ("I wanted to die"). Raising her head means to her a regaining of the ability to assess her overall existential situation rather than being caught up in the immediate consequences of the violence. This assessment is the first sign that now she is proceeding toward "controlling" or taming the violent event, whereas until now, the experience of violence controlled her. This change in her position vis-à-vis the violence is a necessary condition for entering negotiations with her partner. The man intuitively senses the underlying significance of her assessment accordingly and tries to shorten this process. He instinctively grasps that by domesticating the violence, she will be able to transform his lapse into power over him. Once the woman comes to terms with her own experience, she can shift her attention to her partner and take a stand concerning the violence. A woman stated, "I was going to let him know something happened after he beat and kicked me. I was going to bring the police, tell his friends, tell his family so that he could not hide anymore, pretending life goes on." Aware of this turn in the woman's attitude, the batterer strives to stop the process by undermining her strategic advantage: "I really don't understand what she's blaming me for. You could think I did who knows what to her. Did I kill her? I don't know what she'll get out of making me into a monster." The woman figures that her partner is laboring at minimizing and concealing, so she makes it plain she is about to tell the story to a larger audience, and by publishing it, render him unable to deny its full significance. The man views her act of exposing their intimate violence as even more aggressive than the violent act itself and resorts to a naive posture. However, by saying that he does not understand how she can benefit from vilifying him, he also implies that the publicity itself might be to her advantage.

It should be remarked that this prenegotiation assessment time was not uniform in terms of its quality, scope, and duration among the interviewees. By some couples, this reassessment was superficial and short, and they hastened to resume their everyday life: "There is not much to do. . . . We fight, we are mad, we make up." Others lend greater weight to the aftermath by protracting it and increasing it's depth: "After he hits me, it takes us ages to recover. We can go on like that for weeks, everyone is simmering in his own juices."

Negotiating in the Aftermath of Violence

The semantic field of *negotiation* is large and may include one or more of the following elements: to obtain or to arrange by bargain, conference, or agreement; to deal or bargain with someone; to confer with another to arrive at a settlement concerning something (Oxford English Dictionary, 1971). These definitions are so broad that they are of little help in drawing distinctions between various forms of goal attainment among which negotiation is but one. For the purposes of this chapter, we consider negotiations in the aftermath as unique, due to the fact that each partner wants to reestablish we-ness on his or her own terms. In other words, although they both want to arrive at a modus vivendi, they believe this is possible only if they can release themselves from the grip of the other while enhancing their own hold on the other.

The dynamics of negotiating, as we found in our research, involved the women's inclination to open the entire relationship for reexamination. Because women perceive the violence as a symptom of a deteriorating relationship, they believe that the reexamination should be thorough. Such an examination in retrospect would make the violence "worthwhile." In general, for the man, it is best to skip negotiations altogether and go straight back to so-called normal. Accordingly, as has been said, his efforts in the aftermath are directed to trying to minimize the impact of his violence (e.g., by attempting to overcome her tendency to "exaggerate" it). He experiences her resistance to his attempts to normalize the situation as actual violence.

It follows that if the woman agrees to keep the aftermath short, he will interpret this as surrender and is then likely to be violent again.

If she resists it, his wish will be legitimatized as a way of overcoming her resistance and defending himself. The negotiations take place within the dimensions of time and space. The length of the time usually varies according to the duration of the aftermath and the parties' manipulative tampering with the dynamics of the process. The spatial dimension is the social and psychological distance between the partners. The starting point of the aftermath is associated with a gap between the partners. The entire process in the aftermath is an attempt to close this gap. However, conflict is immanent in the contrasting solutions suggested by partners for closing it. The attempts to manipulate the gap can be seen as a mating ritual in which partners end up playing gender-specific roles: She is playing "hard to get" as he sees it, whereas he is "playing with her." Whether the aftermath will lead back to we-ness or not is dependent on whether the couple have the resources to affect a fulfilling rapport between them as they each play their roles in this ritual.

Through the following quotes, we will illustrate the various stages of the negotiation process, beginning with moving from damage control by the woman, expressed in her primary orientation to the violent event, to negotiation, in which her primary orientation is toward returning to normal life. Men play a reactive part in both cases. In the first quote, the woman is seen to be immersed in the violent event. She said,

> I decided to place him under total boycott. I wouldn't sleep with him. I slept with the child. I let him feel that just as I was inferior to him, he'll be a million times more inferior. Just like I am zero for him, he'll be zero for me. Let him feel what I felt. . . . He is trying to kiss me, hug me, get close to me, and I would reject him because it really hurts me and upsets me. . . . After all he did to me, I wouldn't let you sour my life, burn me and then spill water over me.

Her partner described the same process as follows:

> The truth of the matter is that she calms down. She goes to bed and it's over. She's upset 2 or 3 days, she doesn't speak to me and it's over. I never apologize. Never. . . . I don't know if it's through the eyes, or it's from smiles or something, but suddenly everything becomes good, and then it happens again over and over. It's the way it is for the last 7 years.

The woman's experience of the aftermath focuses on the spatial dimension, as she attempts to gain space from her partner to deal with the emotional consequences of the violent event. The man, on the other hand, looks forward rather than backward and focuses on the temporal dimension, believing that the closing of the gap between them is only a matter of time. The woman is conducting an inner dialogue in which she expresses all her frustration and pain in an aggressive manner. However, her aggression turns inward without being inflicted on her partner. This ritual seems familiar to him, and he believes that all he needs to do is to wait her out. Although the woman, from her point of view, is taking revenge by rejecting him and making him experience her plight, the man interprets her as withdrawing into herself temporarily. He needs to absolutely avoid apologizing, as he knows that once she's done with her private ritual, she'll be back together with him. It is obvious from this quote that the woman is active, whereas the man is passive during the aftermath. However, there is variation in the degree of activity-passivity among couples. For instance, in the following quote, the woman is passive, whereas the man attempts to close the gap: "He comes and starts talking and sticks to me. So I answered him. I had no choice. I broke down. What could I do? I said to myself, That's what I've got."

The previously quoted couple had their mind on the violence. This is a temporary stage, because the mutual expectation is to move on. The following quote illustrates the gradual shift from violence to a nonviolent way of life for the couple. The woman said,

> He is trying to make up quickly, very quickly. He'll try to hug me and touch me. I get upset from it, but that's the way he is. . . . I want him to learn and I want to learn that in the future he can't come after an hour, hug me, and think it's all straightened out and whatever happened is forgotten.

On the other hand, the man said,

> My behavior comes from nerves. After an argument, I can kiss her. "Come on honey . . ." and all is in order. . . . Usually, when I calm down, I apologize. . . . I hate being angry with her for long. I'll tell her, "You want to stop the fights? I'll mind my hands and you mind your mouth. . . ." Sometimes, I am to blame, sometimes she is . . . but even then, I prefer to end it and keep it civilized.

The woman quoted here observes the relationship rather than being immersed in the violence, as was our previous informant. This indicates that she is moving away from the violence and is able to contemplate her partner, herself, and their couplehood from a distance. She is now focusing on future scenarios rather than the present. Her ability to adopt an observer's view becomes a source of power and a moral foundation for future scenarios. Nevertheless, instead of completely barring him from future violence, she merely confines herself to determining how he should behave after the next violent event. In other words, the potential for violence continues to be expected and is taken for granted. The negotiation focuses not on whether there will be violence or not but rather on how the next aftermath should be framed in terms of time and space. The woman negotiates for the extent of her control along these two dimensions: She knows what her partner would prefer (short aftermath and quick rapprochement), whereas she wants the opposite (long aftermath and slow rapprochement). The reasons offered by our interviewees by way of explanations of these opposite tendencies varied. Yet the overriding theme among them was the woman's belief that once she achieved control over the scope and rhythm of the aftermath, she would be able to match her partner's control over the violent event. Now, when a man gets an inkling of this, it ironically helps him justify his violence because, by surrendering control during the aftermath, his control by violence is now balanced and thus "justified." The man clarified this in the preceding quote by attributing equal power to his physical and her verbal abuse (e.g., minding his hands and her mouth). Whereas the woman can use her mouth before, during, and after the violence, he can use his hands only at the time of violence. So by allowing her the freedom to use verbal violence any time, his use of physical violence is balanced, at least in his view. Such a construction of reality makes them both "uncivilized," giving him the moral grounds to expect the opposite (e.g., keep it civilized).

The negotiation takes place within the boundaries of the possible. The partners negotiate with a clear expectation of what can be achieved. If nothing can be expected, there is nothing to negotiate. The following quote illustrates the boundaries of negotiation as governed by expectations. A woman said,

> I will remember [the violence] for a long time, but I have to end the settling of accounts. What sense does it make to keep reminding him, for a whole week, that he hit me or swore at me. . . . Our life goes back to normal till further notice.

The partner said,

> I am commenting on what happened, and she tells me her stuff. Finally, I either agree or not, but in general, I am trying not to bring up the topic as I know it just gets on her nerves and this is a pity.

Nothing can be expected between these partners. They seem to know each other well, they tacitly agree on this fact, and thus they come to an unspoken agreement that negotiation makes no sense, so it is better to keep it short.

Other partners had few, if any, expectations from the negotiations but participated anyway as a rite of passage from violence to harmony. In such cases, partners seemed to perform a well-rehearsed "choreography" in which everyone was going through the motions, but there was no affective content. A woman said, "We argue and after several hours we make up . . . as if nothing happened. We know it will continue an hour, two, each one does his thing and then we make up and everything is OK as before." The man said,

> How do we make up? We sit in the evening, "Why did you do that? Why did you do that and that." You are wrong, the other is wrong. At the end, whoever is right is right, whoever is not is not, and whatever happened has happened.

The woman is intent on the duration of the ritual and on restoring things to the way they were before the violence. The man is providing information on the lack of content of the ritual (e.g., doing "this or that" but never saying what). The function of the ritual as a rite of passage alone would not keep it going. But it also enables the partners to lick their wounds and recover from the violence. As one man said, "Time is the best medicine for such things. Not on the same day, usually it doesn't work the same day. Usually, it can be done the next day. We are people that flare up easily and cool off easily." The female partner said, "We don't drag out arguments for a long time, even if it's a serious one. We talk as usual, and we say let's make up." The only medicine needed is a short break. This makes the violence in the man's experience a "mild illness." Such a method makes recovery palpable and quick without need of major intervention. This in turn makes violence insignificant, which, like all minor ailments, comes and goes without a specific reason. Partners remain "healthy" in spite of the violence and can handle it with no apparent difficulty. One flare-up followed by a cooling down should not constitute a major ailment. The woman seems to concur with the meaning attributed to the negotiation by the man. She believes the negotiation is a burden that she shouldn't drag out, for it leads nowhere. Thus, as the partner, she wants to shorten this stage to the minimum and get on with their joint lives.

The somewhat obvious assumption underlying negotiation is that partners negotiate with each other in the form of a dialogue. However, we found that negotiations are not necessarily conducted with the other but at times with oneself. Such so-called negotiations may lead to results that are either accepted or totally unexpected. However, partners neither await the results nor check them with each other but rather take it for granted that the results are those desired by both sides. The following quote is illustrative of a negotiation that is directed at the other:

> He calms down real fast and then he slowly comes close, attempts to reconcile. He attempts to smile with a hug here and there, so I can calm down. He sees that I continue being angry. Sure, I'll stay angry. You can't keep getting beaten and cry and be happy. Being hit, it hurts, and the humiliation and the pain. I think he's trying . . . suddenly he's ready to take me out and stuff: "Let's go out, let's go to a movie . . ." That's how I can tell that he's actually sorry about what he did. That's how he is able to show me.

The preceding quote includes both temporal and spatial dimensions as they are used by partners in the process of reconciliation. There is a process of mutuality and dialogue. The woman knows her man: She knows "he calms down fast." Yet by "coming close slow," he signals that he also knows her and is considerate of her needs. This introduces an element of calm into the negotiation that is based on predictability and mutuality, which sets the stage for courting and rapprochement. The woman continues to keep her options open and understands that the negotiation has not been concluded. Although she can respond to his courting (smiles and hugs) by calming down without bringing the negotiation to an end, she will find no relief for her previous pain and humiliation. As he continues to try, she raises the price and hopes to be compensated by acts (going to the movies) that in themselves have no importance for her unless they can be interpreted as an expression of regret. In other words, in her view, the more he compensates her, the more he regrets the violence. In the woman's experience, there is a double lesson to be learned from the negotiation. First, the man, she knows, will learn that violence has a price. If the price is low, he will continue being violent, but if she succeeds in raising the price in the aftermath, the man will consider it too high and will not be able to afford to be violent in the future. The other lesson she learns is that the more her partner is willing to compensate her, the more he loves her. Her security, lost in the violence, is restored, and they can go on. Understanding the process of reconciliation is more important than it seems, as it inversely reflects the way the woman perceives escalation of violence: Her value in her partner's eyes diminishes, and she is taken for granted. She then believes that she is unlovable and undeserving. He will therefore become violent because of all this and, paradoxically, because he believes violence will change it all around. The processes just described are results of highly visible interactive negotiations. However, such a negotiation can occur latently, as an internal process, between the individual and himself, without the participation of an interlocutor. One man described the negotiation as follows:

> She says nothing, and that's it. We don't get close to one another. I sit still, watch TV. I simmer inside for a while. I keep talking to myself, figuring things out alone. When I am alone, I calm down slowly. . . . I don't go on putting on a show.

The man quoted here combines the effect of distance and time to achieve silence and successfully avoid dialogue with his partner. Not having an external audience enables him to calm down and to process the interpersonal events. By distancing his partner, he gets close to himself. In this way, he expresses that interpersonal relations interfere with authentic inner processes. He uses the TV as a buffer between himself and the woman. Last, the man dichotomizes between inner dialogue, which is authentic, and external dialogue, which he regards as a mere show.

An important aspect of the negotiation process is related to the issue of power, authority, and control. To rate the negotiation as successful, the parties need to experience a certain degree of freedom: freedom of choice, initiative, and approved separateness. The quotes that follow illustrate (a) attempts at achieving a sense of mutuality in the power balance of the first couple and (b) attempts to impose control by the second couple. A woman said,

> At the time of the violence, I wouldn't say anything. Next day, he would come home from work, I wouldn't talk to him either. But after that, we start sending signals; when he would start talking to me, I would start answering. We wouldn't stay mad for a long time.

The man in this couple stated,

> At times, I lose control over myself, I give her a punch in the stomach, in the head . . . real strong. Then, I usually feel she is to blame for it. In the same moment, I can't apologize. But after a couple of hours, I go to her, I court her, touch her, she pretends and plays a bit

since she's hurt . . . then she comes along, and we go back to as if it were normal.

In the aftermath, the woman represents the negotiations in her mind as based on mutuality and choice. She starts out being hurt, but she chooses to achieve reconciliation by exercising her freedom to respond in any way she chooses. Her focus is on the relationship and the need for symmetry in the responses. The man accounts for his violence in terms of loss of control and thus constructs the aftermath as a process of regaining control. This applies to both himself and his partner. He never apologizes, and thus he maintains his sense of control. Within this framework, he chooses to court her and concedes her need for compensation. He perceives her as clay in the hands of the potter and does not take her resistance seriously, as he knows from past experience that it will be overcome. He shapes and recreates her. Last, he knows that he is playing an "as it were" game, but an important one, because it highlights his sense of control. However, not all men tolerate games. A woman said,

> I make up with him since I have no choice. A man like him does not accept that you won't talk to him. He keeps coming at me, teases me, pinches me . . . so I would talk to him. He feels bad, he knows he was bad. Sometimes, I sit and think what does it help me to be angry with him? I must stop, sit and talk it over with him. We talk and he promises. At times, seldom, he promises to calm me down. Inside me, I don't make up. . . . I am trying to overlook things. . . . Perhaps it will improve. . . . I live in the hope it will. . . . He recognizes that he was wrong. This is important. There are men who beat their wives and still think they are OK. He at least recognizes he was wrong.

The man describes the same process as follows:

> I am clear about the fact that I am bad and she is OK. I am aware that I am leading to this. She can scream and talk. . . . I would just shut up since I know she is right. When she's right, I'll let her talk and swear. When I am right, she knows I wouldn't shut up.

The negotiation of the aftermath between the members of this couple is based on coercion. Three themes can be identified in the preceding quote as presented by the woman. First, she establishes that the man is as violent in the aftermath as he was during the violent event (e.g., ". . . coming at me, teases me, pinches me"). Thus, violence is his nature (e.g., "a man like him does not accept . . ."). Second, she accounts for her choice to make up with her partner by the man's regret of the violence he has committed (e.g., "he feels bad, he knows he was bad . . ."), by more violence in the aftermath, and by showing that she weighed the risks and the benefits of making up with him and came to the conclusion that she will gain nothing by resisting (e.g., "what would it help me"). Third, she explains how she can live with him by blocking out the violence in the past (e.g., "trying to overlook things") and clinging to the hope for the future (e.g., "living in the hope it will . . . "). The woman succeeds in reconciling her lack of choice with her need to freely choose by constructing a double reality: She chooses to submit to him. The man's situation is far simpler. He makes the choices and controls the events. There are no gray areas in his experience: He knows who is right and wrong and what the consequences of this situation are in terms of who shuts up and when. He has no doubts concerning his leadership in the given situation.

Partners living in violence will define the negotiations in the aftermath of violence as successful as long as they can create at least an illusion of complementarity. The more successful the partners are in achieving this, the higher the likelihood that the next violence will be postponed. However, this is not always the case. One woman said,

> I left and lived with my parents for a period of time. A man raised his hand to a woman. It seemed strange. So I just picked up my bag and left. I said whatever will happen will happen. He would call daily, but my parents really didn't like it. They thought it was weird. Since they never had it happen between them. It took a month or so. He kept begging and begging, he said he'll be all right, and I decided to come home again.

The man described the same period as follows:

> She told them [her parents] whatever suited her. Instead of them coming and asking what happened, they just heard that I slapped her. They told her right away, "We'll go to the rabbinical court and ask for divorce. And I, . . . what happens with me is that if I am being threatened, I must prove that no one can get me. The first week she said that she'll divorce me. And after a week or two, she forgot what the problem was and started missing me. I wouldn't lie to you, I was missing her too, I was missing her, and for me it was worse since I was missing the kid, too. So her missing me started to work. She found herself between the devil and the deep blue sea since her parents told her, "If you return to him, you are finished with us," and on the other hand, she wants to return to me and in addition, she ran away from home. So how will she come back? Our neighbors and friends tried to talk sense to her and help her to get off the fence and come back. And that's the way it was. She returned

after a month. Actually, she had to run from her parents and come to me.

The woman describes several stages in the negotiation process, which starts with the story of leaving and ends with returning. She accounts for leaving by being surprised by the violence and considering it unusual and unacceptable (e.g., "that a man should raise his hand to a woman . . . seems strange"). Subsequently, she proceeds to account for her returning to her partner by the man's begging and promises (e.g., "he kept begging and begging . . . he said he'll be all right . . ."). To emphasize her decisiveness to leave, she presents herself as willing to take risks (e.g., "whatever will happen will happen") and presents her parents as an important source of support. The more decisive she presents herself to be in leaving, the more her decision to return appears as a free choice.

The man constructs the negotiation in quite the opposite terms. The only points of correspondence between the two narratives are the fact that she left and returned. The man envisions the situation as one of injustice. By blaming the partner's parents for the injustice, he achieves a twofold goal. First, the parent's deadly grip rather than her own choice explain the woman's leaving. Second, he can depict his persuading her to return home as saving her from that grip so that he is a hero and not a wimp. In any case, his violence is out of focus and not an active part of the negotiation. In the final analysis, the partners reconstructed the event in highly divergent terms but succeeded in bringing about the feeling that she is returning to him as a heroine, and he has saved her; it doesn't hurt him, then, to give her a hero's welcome. Still, the question remains, when do these constructs crash against their unacknowledged expectations from each other? For each partner sees the other as indebted: she for pardoning him and he for saving her.

Materializing the Results of Negotiation

Just like the phase of damage control prior to negotiation, the attempts to cash in on the understandings reached through negotiating in the aftermath should not be viewed as a particular period. Rather, they are part of an ongoing process, beginning and culminating in the aftermath. During negotiation, partners develop a series of mutual expectations that epitomize their togetherness, which is possible, assuming no major gap exists between expectations and actualization. The moment the gap arising from the partners' inevitably divergent reconstructions of reality comes into view marks the end of the aftermath as well the potential beginning of the next violent event. As one man said,

> I got to the point that I was feeling that everything is back to normal, but again, she is stretching the rope too much. . . . She always does that. It teaches you that you shouldn't be too good. When you're good, it goes up to her head.

The woman said, "After all we've been through, I expected a little more. But I remained naive, and he didn't shed his old skin." Partners rediscover at this stage what they already knew about each other. This is a stage of awakening and sobriety associated with much disenchantment. The woman senses that her partner failed to deliver on his promise, whereas the man believes she has long overdrawn her account. She is perceived as greedy and he as stingy. If he lets her continue, their relationship will go bankrupt. He must stop her. His attempts to do this present him as ever greedier. The seeds of escalation are planted in the aftermath.

Summary

We have shown in this chapter that the aftermath of violence becomes a mirror of the violent event. Most partners succeed in reconstructing the aftermath as a period suffused with hope. When they rediscover the violence after the aftermath, the latter becomes "paradise lost," highlighting not only their disenchantment and entrapment but also the inexorable inevitability of the Sisyphean and tantalizing, perpetual search for it. The aftermath primarily connotes destruction, yet it is always remembered in the couple's collective mythology as a time of reconciliation and closeness. The memory of violence and that of the aftermath balance each other. But whereas the constitution of violence tends to be factual, that of the aftermath is virtual. When the distinction stares them in the face, the partners continue searching for paradise lost from the depths of the hell where they dwell.

4

Scripts of Everyday Life

This chapter describes and analyzes the day-to-day life of couples living in violence. We will show the dynamics of everyday life, ranging from order and certainty at one end, to chaos and unpredictability at the other. Intimate violence occurs within the routine of daily chores, economic decisions, child rearing, relationship with the extended family, recreational activities, and so on. While everyday life goes on, each one of the spouses forms a new evaluation of their togetherness. To understand the daily routine of these couples, we must take note of the expression of their general evaluations in their descriptions of their lives together and in their expectations regarding their couplehood.

Order and Predictability in Everyday Life

To make joint life possible, partners in violence organize their life and attempt to make it orderly and predictable. But our contention is that the particular ways in which they structure and give content to this order inevitably lead to increased disorganization and unpredictability.

Rigid gender roles determine and organize these couples' togetherness. Although these gender roles seem to be universal, their rigidity is unique to couples living in violence. It stems from the fact that they not only serve as a framework but as a step-by-step user's guide for everyday life, which allows no space for negotiation or dialogue. Because the partners view the structure of their couplehood as highly vulnerable, and the rigid gender roles are experienced as the sole anchor of security and predictability, any attempt to negotiate these roles is viewed as threatening the relationship as a whole. One woman stated,

> I do all the chores around the house. My husband is working and supports the house, and I take care of the children, do the house, everything. No work division. That is to say, I run the house, I know it all. Sometimes when I clean, he plays with the children. But over-all, I do everything, and I keep up the house.

Her partner depicted essentially the same reality:

> Without any formal agreement, my role is to make sure that there is everything in the house; whether I work or not, it doesn't matter, I have to make sure there is everything and find solutions. So that we have enough to cover our debts and we have food and stuff . . . so our existence is ensured.

These quotes illustrate the status quo in a seemingly normal life, which is based on a well-rehearsed prescriptive scenario reflecting rigid gender distribution of duties and responsibilities. Emphasis is on exclusive territoriality and its symbolic connotations: Everything related to work outside the house is the man's province and a symbolic anchor of loyalty to a set of prescribed values. Similarly, everything related to the family and its internal concerns is the woman's responsi-bility, symbolizing her commitment and loyalty. These two realities seem to be complementary and mutually reinforcing. It also appears that both the woman and the man accept this division and deem it the authoritative basis of their power and status. Both partners describe a situation in which division of labor is based on results and is indepen-dent of how the results are achieved (e.g., "whether I work or not"). The man is expected to provide for the household from external resources, and the woman is expected to make the most of the income toward the family welfare. They evaluate each other according to the degree of fulfillment of these expectations. Exactly how the one goes about meeting these requirements is of little moment to the other. Partnership in such a venture is avoided, for this would imply mutual responsibility, which might blur the agreed-on gender role boundaries. The tacit awareness that any infringement of these arrangements will lead to conflict can be inferred from the following quote:

> I came back from work tired and hungry, and I didn't find her there. There was no food either. So I got pissed off. The force of habit . . . I am used to find her and to find food. You are controlled by your habit, and suddenly you don't get what you're used to.

His partner said,

> He asked me, "Why did you go out? Why won't you stay home?" He likes it that when he comes from work, I sit at home with the kids, sit with him and have a meal. If he comes and doesn't find me at home, he wouldn't set the table himself or eat alone. He wouldn't eat until I get home, and sometimes it bores me to stay home all day. . . . I get upset from this stuff. If I get the food ready and leave it ready, I don't see any reason to argue about this, but it seems that such things are a good reason to argue for him.

The man perceives himself as abiding by the contract by going to work. When he returns home, his side of the contract is fulfilled. Being tired and hungry is a testimony to his exhaustive use of his resources to keep his side of the contract. His social image is positive and his self-esteem high. He is now in a position to evaluate and judge his partner's performance at home, on the basis of his expectations, formed through habit and therefore taken for granted. Whereas he evaluates his input (i.e., he went to work) without going into the details of whether the output of his work is satisfactory (i.e., whether he made enough money to keep the family going), he evaluates his wife's output in great detail: Is there food? Is she at home? Is she eating with him? and so forth. Furthermore, whereas the man's outputs are presented as measurable and quantifiable, the woman's are more difficult to measure and quantify (e.g., Is the food tasty? Is her company at the table pleasurable?). The criteria for measurement are determined by the man who alone knows them and can thus manipulate them situationally. He positions himself as the "quality controller" of the family and the norm setter who fixes both the expectations and the ways to assess whether they have been met. The woman echoes the man's expectations by quoting his questions concerning what she should do and didn't and so validates his expectations. She understands that the man will never enter her territory (e.g., "he wouldn't set himself the table"). She begins to protest against the existing order (e.g., "I get upset from this stuff"). Both the man and the woman feel dissatisfied

and exploited by one another. The woman further understands that
the man holds the key to the mutual expectations, yet evinces further
flexibility concerning them ("I don't see any reason to argue about
this"). She realizes that her attempts to relax the standards constitute a
challenge, which is likely to be interpreted by him as an encroachment
of his territory as the norm setter and quality manager, roles that are
socially assigned to him as a man. At this point, the organization of
their joint life is disrupted and becomes the source of stress. This is
reflected in the following typical couple dynamics:

> **Male partner:**   I am pressuring her in terms of cleanliness and
> order. I like a clean house, tidy, organized, everything in its
> place. I can't tolerate it when something is not orderly. This is
> like my sickness. But I believe it is a good sickness. A woman
> doesn't always like to arrange everything all the way.
>
> **Interviewer:**   And how does this lead to arguments?
>
> **Male partner:**   There are no arguments. I am right. But she
> doesn't always do what I tell her. . . . What am I expecting? I
> don't expect anything unusual or strange. I am demanding,
> and I believe it's normal. What I demand, it's beautiful and
> desirable. I am unwilling to live in a place which is disorganized.
>
> **Woman partner:**   He says he is working outside, he comes home
> upset, and he wants to have peace and quiet at home, he wants
> the home to be clean and organized, to have food and every-
> thing. This is what counts for him, plus that the children do
> well in school. He's got great expectations, and they are not
> always fulfilled. . . . I think he's really devoted to the house.
> He really cares about the material parts of the household.
> Everything. . . . But interpersonal relations don't count. I sim-
> ply don't feel anything. . . . Not that I am angry or anything,
> but I look at the whole scene and the atmosphere and say that
> he is suffering, too. It is possible that he is suffering, too. He
> expects things and doesn't get them.

The man here is emphasizing order as the supreme value to be hon-
ored for the well-being of the couple, whereas the woman is focusing
on the way they *relate* to each other. This is more important than it
may seem because it reflects a hierarchy among competing values.
Both of them seem dissatisfied with their lives, yet they give opposite
reasons for this. The man believes that the problems in the relationship are caused by his partner's failure to live up to their agreements,

and his solution is to rigidify those. The woman traces the problems to excessive rigidity in her partner's expectations and believes the solution to be in making those more flexible. The man quoted here conceives himself as the sentry in charge of order and tidiness. His measurement criterion is his own tolerance and his tool is pressure. By such self-appointment, the man makes his demands nonnegotiable and his righteousness irreproachable (e.g., ". . . there are no arguments . . . I am right . . I demand"). On the basis of his criticisms of his wife, he leaps to a generalization about the shortcomings of womankind: their tendency to be superficial, cut corners, and be nonsubmissive (e.g., "a woman doesn't always like to arrange everything all the way"). By this ploy, his partner comes to represent her gender, and his essential need to be a sentinel is reinforced. His demands are not merely normative but also acquire aesthetic qualities (e.g., "it's beautiful and desirable").

The normalcy of his demands and his unwillingness to compromise are underscored by his awareness that they may be perceived as "sick," but he defines this as a "good sickness." The use of the sickness metaphor helps the man fulfill his need for inner order and not only environmental order. Under these circumstances, he feels no need to account for his posture in terms of his performance as compared to his partner's. The woman, on the other hand, starts out by implicitly questioning her partner's performance (e.g., "he says he's working outside"). She doesn't know what he really does outside; what she does know is that whatever happens out there brings him back home upset and demanding. She knows his expectations of order (e.g., "he wants the house clean and neat") and translates these into a need for "peace and quiet at home." At the same time, she conveys that such exaggerated expectations are bound to remain unfulfilled. Along with this pessimism, she appreciates his qualities (e.g., "I think he's really devoted to the house"). She has now rendered a balanced picture of her partner. This will serve as the background for her central argument about his lack of interest in their relationship and the effect this has on them (e.g., "I don't feel anything . . . he is suffering too"). She brings the various aspects of her assessment of their problem together at the end of the quote by clarifying that his exaggerated expectations leave no room for personal interaction, for their relationship, and in this way, they constitute the main source of their problems (e.g., "he expects things and doesn't get them").

This analysis strongly suggests that the man is focused on power and control, whereas the woman is profoundly interested in relating. They both account for their positions by differential value hierarchies. These accounts serve to bridge the gap between expectations and

actual behaviors deemed undesirable. There is a crack in the relationship. The man wants to close it and make it disappear, whereas the
woman strives to broaden it into a sufficiently large space for what she
values. The opposing forces at work unsettle the accepted order in the
couple's life. The man continues to stick to the idea that everything is
under control and that the old understandings still work. He refuses to
recognize that underneath this layer of old understandings, business is
not as usual. The woman begins to reconsider old agreements and
their bearing on her life:

> Most of the work is on me. . . . He makes sure that I do the work
> properly. If he sees that I don't do it right, he comments on it. . . . I
> told him there are things that I don't like doing, even if they are
> things at home. I do things not out of love or because I feel like it. I
> do them against my will. Am I a slave or what? He says: "If you just
> do what I tell you, everything will be just fine between us."

Her partner stated,

> She is working at home, cleans and cooks, cares for the children, and
> I work outside, do all the shopping, pay all the bills, everything that
> needs to be done outside, I do. This fits me well, since I have no time
> to do anything at home except some small repair work. . . . When I
> get home from work I am finished.

The woman expresses her dissatisfaction arising from this division of
labor. First, she feels that the load is unbalanced (e.g., "most of the
work is on me"). Second, she is unhappy with the hierarchy according
to which she is a mere laborer and her spouse is her supervisor (e.g.,
"he makes sure that I do the work properly"). The situation is exacerbated by her belief that this hierarchy will perpetuate or increase the
load, depending on her partner's decision. Moreover, her experience
has shown her that any attempt to alleviate the load or alter the hierarchy will be frowned on. Her previous attempts to make marginal
adjustments proved ineffective, so now she seems ready for face-to-
face negotiations about role division. As a first step, she introduces a
new variable into the old framework, work satisfaction (e.g., "I told
him there are things that I don't like doing even if they are things at
home"), and wants to make it a legitimate expectation. She is willing
to continue with the existing role division but presents satisfaction as
an additional condition. Needless to say, although the new demand is
not presented as conflicting with the established order, by its mere
introduction, the balance is changed. Liberating herself in principle

from doing "things against her will" while still recognizing that they have to be done, she creates a situation in which the partner must take her satisfaction into account when negotiating role division. Cleaning the house, or other household chores, must become satisfying or else they won't get done.

By reframing the expectations as described here, the woman does not free herself from her partner's grip but rather attempts to get a grip on him as well. Her question "Am I a slave?" can now be answered by saying "yes." But if she remains one, he is now one, too. At the end of the quote, it becomes clear that in the woman's view, the man is unwilling to change the existing arrangements, and her attempts to negotiate are thwarted. Implicit in his saying that if she will "just do what he tells her, everything will be fine between them" is the indirect threat that a refusal on her part will lead to the opposite results. By quoting her partner's threat, she evinces the understanding that she is in danger, seeing that changes in her expectations have a price. It should be said that though the woman presents the changes in the suggestive mode, for the man, it is as if they are actually occurring, because their mere suggestion is a symptom of the change in the power balance. From the woman's perspective, nothing has changed; all there were were mere ideas; but the very entertaining of such ideas leaves the man no choice but to react. The man's words begin with a description of the role division and the daily expectations the partners have for one another. She does all the work at home, and he performs duties outside the home. He expresses his satisfaction with this state of affairs (e.g., "this fits me well"). He formulates this status quo in terms of limited ability rather than control (e.g., "I have no time to do anything at home . . .").

Moreover, he shows a willingness to do more, if unhampered; doing repair work is testimony to his good intentions (e.g., ". . . except some small repair work"). The man accounts for the role division in terms of time limitations imposed by his duties abroad, and when need be, he adds the exhaustion arising therefrom. By offering accounts that show him as doing as much on his own as he possibly can, he seems to be saying, What I do not do, I cannot do, and what I do, I do out of shear good will. By exhausting his time and physical resources, the man further signals that he takes his outside duties seriously, carrying them out thoroughly (e.g., ". . . I am finished . . ."). The man's message is clear: We have a good arrangement, I like it, and even if we would want to change it, it would be impossible. What is excluded from his message is the question of whether the arrangement is satisfactory to his partner.

Whereas in the previous dialogue we illustrated the woman's attempts to question her own role performance within the boundaries of her territory, the following quote demonstrates a shift in her focus to the man's territory and roles. Finances and banking is the case in point:

> **Woman:**   He controls the entire financial part of our life. He doesn't even allow me to come close to the bank, and he gets angry when I try. He threatens me if I come close to the bank. . . . He once told me he'd shame me if I went there.
>
> **Interviewer:**   Would you want to have the responsibility?
>
> **Woman:**   I don't know anymore. Actually, it's quite comfortable the way it is, even though people tell me that if something should happen, God forbid, I'll be in big trouble. I wouldn't even know what to do. That's true but he wants no part of me in that stuff. . . . I tried several times to convince him, since I really would like to know how to handle it if something should happen to him, but it's impossible to get him to do it.

The woman's opening statement includes several themes. First, she chooses to fragment their joint life into departments (e.g., "the entire financial part of our life"). Second, she speaks in terms of "our life," leaving the we-ness intact. Third, the we-ness within the man's realm is presented as a function of control rather than of partnership. Her attempts to propose any change in the situation (e.g., "to come close to the bank"), encounter his resistance and anger (e.g., "I try . . . he would not allow me"). He threatens but uses emotional rather than physical measures (e.g., to shame her). By shaming her as a form of retaliation, the man indirectly hints that her attempts to interfere with his role brings shame on him. As for her part, he is touchy about her entering the man's territory. On the one hand, she can live with the "comfortable" situation of not having an extra chore, whereas on the other, she feels her ignorance concerning banking is dangerous—not because of its potential to control her but because he may die and take this knowledge to the grave. Because she understands that even hinting at his death may be interpreted as wishful thinking, she is quick to distance herself from it (e.g., "God forbid . . . and people say . . ."). But strikingly, by staying ambivalent, the woman enables herself to experience "choice": She can remain comfortable at the present time by staying out of his territory or else endanger herself by entering into his domain to gain "forbidden" knowledge should anything happen to him. The narrative of her dilemma has been reframed by the woman in terms of long-term versus short-term goals. She can rest in comfort in the present while leaving her options open for the future. She can plan ahead and see the present. At the same time, he is focused on maximizing the present only. Such narrow-mindedness calls for action. A woman who decided to act said,

> In the past, I belonged inside the house. . . . He would do the shopping without me. A few years back, I started to realize that my territory is becoming smaller and smaller. And I started to do the shopping alone myself. He was really upset and offended, and we had endless arguments about this.

In response to this, the partner said, "We don't do the shopping together, in spite of the fact that I demanded to be part of it. But at some point, I pulled back and gave up." The woman provides historical background to explain her decision to act. The territory carved out by her partner for her began to "own" her (e.g., "I belonged inside the house"), and anything outside the house, including shopping, was controlled by her partner. The turning point was her realization that her territory was not only small but was shrinking (e.g., "my territory is becoming smaller and smaller"). She presents few details about the process of change in the form of "endless arguments." The change is sudden and introduced without warning: "I started to do the shopping alone." *Alone* is emphasized by adding "myself," which underscores the need to give such independent behavior high visibility. The man provides a similar narrative in factual terms; however, as the starting point, he chooses the fact that they used to shop together. From that point on, the process described by him is one of retreat both in territory and authority. He gives up. Both narratives move from we-ness to separateness. But whereas the woman's individuality symbolizes a victory, for the man, it embodies defeat. It is as if she has gained "his" independence, hence he has lost "it."

We have shown so far that the partners' attempts to negotiate order through a clear definition of roles and territories leads to further disorder. Although the burden of order may have been unsatisfactory, it provided the couple with boundaries, a sense of predictability, and thus, security. Disorder, as the inevitable outcome of the kind of order they knew, blurs the boundaries and makes the territories permeable but carries with it the hope for a renewed order. Such creation of disorder within a situation of loss of boundaries may exist among conflictual couples but is more pervasive and dramatic among couples living in violence.

Disorder and Unpredictability in Everyday Life

There is no clear-cut separation between order and disorder in the lives of couples living in violence. We have chosen to demarcate them at this point in the chapter for analytic purposes, because the interview material shows that challenges to the existing order are often translated into action.

Most couples, when the old regime was challenged, attempted to confront their versions of the meaning of their past, present, and future. The versions at this stage are different, to the point of total opposition, as illustrated by the following couple. The woman views their life as constantly improving: "The relationship is somewhat better than it was, since we learned from each other. We know what each one likes . . . we learned to get used to it." The man holds a diametrically opposite position:

> I don't think Dorith [his partner] knows how couples should be. A good couple would remain together in fire and water. . . . I see no future in the relationship since Dorith has these terrible mood swings. I can tell you that I am all for a harmonious life, to make the family grow, to have a big family where everyone grows.

The woman reviews the couplehood diachronically, whereas the man reviews it from the present. She perceives a positive trend of improvement stemming from their knowledge of each other (e.g., " we learned from each other"; "we know what each one likes"). The man concedes the fact that there was closeness but believes it to be a negative factor. He has come to know that his partner has no idea about living as a couple and goes as far as to cast doubt as to her sanity (e.g., "terrible mood swings"). These together bring him to the conclusion that the relationship has no hope or future. Unlike previous situations, when the power struggle and the negotiations took place within the boundaries of couplehood, such hopelessness threatens the continuation of joint life itself. The man is now threatening to leave, whereas the woman does not view this as a realistic possibility. Sooner or later, she will come to realize what is happening, and they will both agree that there is no communication between them. The following quote illustrates how the couple faces their loss of communication. The woman said,

> We have no common language. That's all, we have nothing to talk about. I understand things one way, and he understands them another. . . . He simply never agrees with me. So I get discouraged

and am not looking to talk to him anymore. I prefer to talk with someone else. At times, something happens to me on the street, and I really want to tell him about it and hear what he thinks, what his opinion is. But I can't tell him since his reactions are really unpleasant.

The man said,

At times, I talk to her just to show her I am talking to her. But actually, I am uninterested. . . . I would catch myself, I would just be a hypocrite with her, just to give her the good feeling, I would try to talk to her. This is what we really need. I guess if we would really talk seriously, we would enjoy it, and we would love each other more.

Both partners describe their yearning for communication. Whereas the woman is searching to supplement for this lack of communication by seeking contact outside the family (e.g., "I prefer to talk with someone else outside"), the man resorts to pseudocommunication (e.g., "I would just be a hypocrite with her"). Partners give divergent accounts of the lack of communication between them. The woman accounts for it by the loss of a common language, mutual interests, and by general disagreement. The consequence is that she has lost interest in communicating with him at all. Now, what for the woman constitutes the result of the loss of communication, for the man is its cause. Whereas the woman solves her problem by communicating with others outside the family, the man takes to pseudocommunication.

The loss of communication is neither sudden nor can it be fixed at a specific point in time. This continuous process leads to an ever-widening gulf between the partners, which culminates in complete estrangement. A woman said,

He is totally uninvolved in my life. He has no clue how I live and what I do. I live my life, alone. . . . I do everything alone. . . . I really envy those who can cooperate. My heart is broken. I look at other couples. . . . I don't envy them in any mean way, but I envy them because they have it, that it's possible. I see it and I find it so weird. It's such fun. I don't know how would he take this kind of relationship. To a large extent, I don't appreciate him.

Her partner stated,

It could be that in the final analysis, we got used to this situation. Each continues as if he were in the same framework, and he'll build himself his own defenses. . . . With time, a situation of alienation will emerge, and each one will lock himself up in his own world. Perhaps, it was comfortable for me with this arrangement. When I woke up, I knew the situation wasn't comfortable but locked myself into it and continued living. But once you're exposed, you know your situation, and the frustration comes.

The variations in these quotes center on the varying degrees of facing and accepting the ever-increasing gulf between the partners. The woman is facing reality in a highly emotional fashion (e.g., "my heart is broken"), which reflects an overall unwillingness to accept the gulf between herself and her partner. She describes her experience as a sequence of alienation, total separation, and ultimate loneliness. Comparison with others whom she considers normal only deepens her sense of loss. The circle of loss is widening from loss of communication through loss of we-ness, loss of the love and appreciation of the partner, to ultimate loss of hope. Unlike the woman's tendency to face the reality of the situation and without being able to accept it, the man tends to adjust (e.g., "got used to this situation") by creating an alternative reality, which he defines as unreal (e.g., "as if he were in the same framework"). He splits asunder into the unreality of their joint life and the reality of his own. The product of the creation of these parallel realities is an alienation that will inevitably consolidate more and more (e.g., "everyone will lock himself up in his own world"). As long as he succeeds in keeping the alienation outside the focus of his awareness, the situation is endurable, but once he fastens on it, he will reach a position similar to his partner's, and life will become untenable.

When order is lost, partners run out of justifications and excuses and are unable to maintain even a pseudo-order. The relationship disintegrates. There is a sense of impending chaos. A woman said,

> I am always living from one day to the next. It could be that tonight, he'll beat me. I don't see this place as permanent. I know that one day it will all fall apart. 'Cause, this situation cannot continue.

Her partner agreed:

> At times, I see myself falling apart. Just to get rid of the responsibility, I will fall apart. She can get payments from the National Insurance, and I'll manage. . . . The solution is close to me. I feel the divorce is coming. I feel . . . I can bet you 99% that we are getting there.

Both partners are aware that the end of the relationship is in sight, and this is an essential part of their present "togetherness." They express it as unpredictability and detachment (the woman), or as relief from responsibility (the man), but both live in the paradox of predicting the divorce from the unpredictable dyadic relationship. There is a high level of passivity in the way partners talk about their future. They seem to choose to be spectators of the collapse, and the only active components in their attitudes are their negative predictions. The woman seems to have given up on the relationship, does or says nothing to stop the violence, and views the divorce as a way to stop it. The man views the divorce as a solution to his problem without relating it to his violence or to the woman's experience of it.

For many couples, divorce is indeed the solution. Because this was not the choice of the couples we interviewed, at least at the time of the data collection, and because they agreed on the fact that the existing situation was untenable, we need to examine the ways in which they continued their chaotic joint life.

The Order in the Disorder

Partners are caught in their ongoing life patterns and experiences, which have taught them that dramatic changes cannot be expected. The chaos is a given, and the only hope is to domesticate it and make it manageable. To this end, men and women reduce each other to a single core characteristic. By doing so, they are able to understand and predict each other's moves and gain a sense of competence in their own reactions toward the other. One man said,

> I know, and she can't hide it, and I am not embarrassed to say it even though she's my wife, that she behaves in a petty and childish manner. The appropriate terms would actually be stupid. Real stupid and childlike.

Similarly, the woman said,

> Avi's [her partner's] character is such that he is stubborn like hell. He never gives in. Sometimes, if he thinks I didn't behave as he expected, he is capable to get back at me and not to hold his promises. But I don't hold a grudge against him over what he didn't do. . . . He thinks I keep grudges, but that's simply not true.

From the man's perspective, the situation is transparent (e.g., "I know, and she can't hide it"). The shift in the relationship is marked by the visibility of the partner's "real personality." Also, there is a parallel emotional shift ("I am not embarrassed") that feeds into presenting the partner as "real stupid and childlike." By stating that he maintains this opinion of her "even though she is his wife," he distances himself from her and avoids the possibility that the attributed characteristics of his partner will reflect on him. She is now simply a stupid child who needs to be handled appropriately.

The woman presents her partner as stubborn. This characterization has general implications, as well as some that are specifically related to her. His stubbornness is presented as characterological rather than situational (i.e., unrelated to her or to her behavior). By so doing, she reduces him to stubbornness and distances herself from him just as he did from her. Both partners narrowed each other down to single descriptive characteristic. They created a safe distance between them and constructed a situation in which whatever one of them did was attributed to their respective stupidity or stubbornness.

Whereas the partners were firm in their respective perceptions of each other, they never accepted the other's perceptions of them. The following quotes are illustrative. One man said,

> I have a way of life that we agreed on, before we got married. And after we got married, there was no agreement from her. She is trying to change things around. She can't break me. . . . She's got a whole different mentality than she used to have before the wedding. . . . She got me and that's it. It's like when someone wants to get something and once she's got it, throws it into the closet. She simply has no appreciation for me.

The woman said,

> I didn't change. I am the same simple woman. But he sees me differently. He switched eyeglasses. . . . Sometimes, what hurts me is not the slap, the problem is that I am exposed, I can't defend myself. This is not the ideal of our life. 'Cause I was thinking I am married to this fine delicate gentleman. I wasn't about to get dragged into the marriage by all means, like these other women. I wanted this because I thought we had a good thing going. He changed a great deal, he changed horribly. I really have serious reservations about him; this is not the same man I used to love . . . this is not the same person. I want him to leave me alone and let me live my life.

Both partners maintain that they didn't change (e.g., the woman: "I didn't change"; the man: "she can't break me") but that their partners had changed since the wedding. Entailed by the perception of change is the sense of having been cheated (e.g., the woman: "He switched eyeglasses"; the man: "She's got a whole different mentality"). The other's true nature was unveiled. They both present the partner's revealed personality as a disappointing discovery rather than as a result of an interactive process.

The unfulfilled expectations can be overcome by each playacting the role expected. The following description of the couple's sex life is a case in point. One man said,

> I want her in bed, and therefore, I am trying to make up with her. Sometimes, I tell her to play, play roles in bed. Pretend. . . . I want to get it off. Let me help you, I'll do whatever you want me to.

The woman said about the same issue, "There are times I force myself to do it. It's not that he forces me . . . I force myself to keep him happy in order to shut him up and hopefully things will get better." The only expectation left is that the partners pretend, be unreal, play roles, force themselves, to satisfy the immediate needs of the other. Thus, faking and pretending intimacy becomes a permanent feature of the relationship, providing an added dimension to the "as-if-ness" of it. Faking becomes the official means for dyadic transactions: The woman fakes sex to buy silence; the man is willing to have his partner fake intimacy to buy sex. Partners need to live in the make-believe world they have created and of which they are aware. To live with such awareness, there is a need for a renewed commitment. Fakeness becomes the method for maintaining togetherness as a means toward socially acceptable goals, such as "for the kids' sake." A man said,

> Sometimes, I feel like waking up tomorrow and going to court to finish this whole ordeal. . . . Sell everything and everyone on the way, go to our parents or something. She wants to show that she's not afraid. She'd say, "No problems, let's do it and get it over with." On the other hand, I tell her, if we didn't have the kid, I would get up and leave. The only thing that keeps me is the child . . . and I am afraid of breaking up the family nest, the child, the home I started. I often wonder, I sit and think one way or the other. . . . Let's see, perhaps it'll get better, I keep hoping it will get better, perhaps later, perhaps in a month or two. Perhaps, the situation will improve.

His wife said,

> Sometimes, I would give up. There is no chance he will change. It's better to end it right there. But then I think that if I would go to court, this would pressure him. He would say "I don't want to divorce, to ruin the family, the child, I would take any job." But it

doesn't work, there are no such results. . . . The child is the only
thing which connects us in many ways. . . . It's our light, our lamp.

For both partners, the child is identified as the last source of joint
meaning. The "best interest of the child" doctrine is a socially acceptable and even laudable goal. As such, it radiates authenticity on the
entire relationship. Being "child savers," they cannot consider themselves simply as fakers. Their attempt to remain a family becomes real
in their experience, bringing hope to the entire family system. Hope
creates expectations: He will provide for the children, and she will
take care of them. We are back to the gender roles we started with.

Summary

We have attempted to describe and analyze the dynamics of the
everyday life of partners living in violence. We have shown their struggles to construct an orderly world, deal with chaos arising from those
attempts, and reconstruct another order. We have analyzed this continuous process from the couples' rigid adaptation of familiar social
scripts, such as gender roles and expectations. The rigid adherence to
these scripts brings the family to the brink of chaos and collapse,
which gives rise to the experience of "losing the script." From that
point on, they are in search of their lost script. Should they find it, old
agreements can be renewed, and life will resume its course. If they
don't, their joint life has no meaning.

5

From Emotions
in Violence to
Violent Emotions

Intimate violence is a highly emotional phenomenon, and therefore, it cannot be fully understood without examining its emotional base (Denzin, 1984, 1989). It is well confirmed that the experience of acting violently is invariably accompanied by a deep sense of loss. Of course, every loss is a loss of what was "mine." For the violent man, the loss is not only of love but also of the ability to control his partner. Paradoxically, continuous violence reiterates for him the ever-increasing loss inherent in trying to regain her by force. For the woman, violence is loss of love, trust, and hope. Clearly, these losses are not easily recoupable for either of them. They have both lost positive feelings and experience the need to face negative emotions that become a constant feature of their relationship. For those who remain together in spite of violence, there is an acute awareness of the loss and negative emotions, as well as the necessity to bridge with oneself and the other between violence and togetherness. How can the story of their emotional biography continue?

We examined our interview material to answer the question of how negative and positive emotions can coexist in intimate violence. In trying to answer this question, let us begin by examining love and guilt, which play important roles in understanding intimate violence. On the basis of these key emotions, we propose a theoretical model of the emotions that occur in violence. We consider them as fruitful in exploring other emotions beyond the specific ones used to illustrate the model.

Love

Through love, people come to know themselves, their own essence, and that of the other. It could be said then, leaping to the generalization, that emotions are vital to the way we know the world. The process of knowledge acquisition involves three stages: First, people become self-aware, and then they define their emotions; second, they experience emotions in the light of their definition; and third, through emotional experience, they define their existence in the world. These layers of emotionality are present at any given time in the development of the emotion, but the focus changes as the process unfolds. That is, it may be that in the initial stages, the focus is on defining the emotion, and later, it can move to experiencing and giving meaning to it. A battered woman defined her emotion, as illustrated by the following quote:

> When it started, we literally "fell" on each other. We didn't even know each other, and right from the beginning it was very romantic. . . . For about half a year, he would just look at me and say nothing, never came to me or anything. . . . I noticed it, but he wasn't the only one, so I didn't pay attention. And then he turned to me accidentally and everything else happened real fast. After a week, we went out, and the same evening, we went to bed, and it was clear that there is a very strong commitment. So it was like a strong click, I would say explosive. . . . The next 3 months, our togetherness was real intensive . . . the entire phase of getting to know each other was not gradual and slow but rather sudden. It was clear from the beginning, in a week or two, that we would get married since we want to be together. In 3 months, we decided to live together. That's it. Then it slowly got into a routine and things got normalized. . . . You know it wasn't normal life when we were living in each other's ass, and when that stopped, the difficulties started.

This woman defines love as personal advantage and ownership: She acquired something that she didn't have previously. Metaphors such as "falling" or "being in each other's ass" signal the receiving of a significant other into one's own individual space. The emotions are directed toward oneself. She is not in love with the other but rather with herself-in-love. The experience is one of sudden ("explosive") change in spatial arrangements between the partners, one of sensual intoxication. Immediately following this transformation, the woman uses commitment as a way of building a "fence" around the newly created joint space. Rushing into sex is one way of achieving this. When possession is confirmed, each one of the partners develops a sense of security. Once this happens, things can go back to normal, and togetherness is routinized and can be understood in normative terms. Such a normalization is a precondition to transferring the emotion from the personal to the interpersonal sphere. Only following this process can the woman reflect on the emotion and share it with others. The man's description is shorter but essentially similar: "Let me see. . . . In the beginning, our couplehood was based mostly on sex, to overcome loneliness. With time, it changed, it came to emphasize friendship and commitment. That's about it." By using the term "overcoming loneliness" through a physical act such as sex, the man symbolically performs the same "receiving" act as the one described by his partner. Subsequently, the fenced-in joint space is sanctioned by commitment, just as the woman says. The potential of loss is inherent in such a strong commitment to owing the other, and the physical means to enforce it are the seeds of violence, once the threat of loss becomes imminent.

In the next stage in the development of the emotion, emphasis is placed on its routinization and integration into everyday existence. One woman described this stage as follows:

> And then all hell broke lose. I should say there was some of it before, too, but after a while, there is love, and there are all the compromises that need to be made. And then we got to real hard fights, arguments, and in the meantime, we decided to get married. After a while, we went into therapy, we got to understand many things, many ways in which we complement each other. It was a good beginning, but not enough. Everyone accepts the other, as it were, there is more willingness to accept each other. . . . Everyone uses the other to reduce tensions. We bring all the tensions home, and this often creates very difficult situations. That's why we argued on Saturday. . . . And when this happens, everything explodes at home. That's my interpretation of the situation. Our love is built layers on layers, and I have lots of hope.

At this point in the relationship, the partners turn to each other, they shift the focus from themselves to the other and to their togetherness. If love was seen previously as aimed at overcoming loneliness, now they expect to get something out of their togetherness. Such a transition is associated with difficulties as expressed in fights and compromises to be made. Obviously, the partners believe that this is a normal state of affairs because they sealed it by marriage. This may further be functional in overcoming the threats to security arising from arguments and compromises inherent in attempting to "accommodate" each other. At this stage, love is defined as being together with one another. It is expected to be experienced as "joint welfare," in the sense that each one of them enhances the welfare of the other through complementarity. They interpret this situation along the lines of "two are better than one" (a Hebrew proverb), and frame it in utilitarian terms: There is something to gain from being together. One man said: "Love is getting together. It gives more security, more power, it will to do more for me and my family. And there is a reason to live." The expectations of benefits and the potential for disillusionment are both high. When love is defined and experienced through meaning by its benefits, there is actually nothing other oriented in it. Thus, although this stage is seemingly oriented toward togetherness, it remains as self-centered as the previous one. Violence is likely to result from the gap between what the partners expected to get out of being together and what actually occurs in their everyday existence.

The next stage in the development of love is one in which partners move from joint welfare to growth. It is expected here that the partners will attain higher levels of self-realization, individually and together. Although most partners living in violence know about the existence of this stage in principle (e.g., there is hope in the "layers of love"), they never actualize it, because they are stuck in the disillusionment arising from the previous stage, and thus violence substitutes for it.

So far, we have described and illustrated the structure and content of love as a framework for couplehood. We have shown how partners define emotions in the context of emotional awareness and how they experience love and give meaning to it. We suggest that the need to achieve security and personal gain through this emotion and the pursuit of these needs sows the seeds of violence. We can now proceed to understand the experience of loving the other and being loved.

Loving and Being Loved in Violence

To the questions, "Do you love your partner?" and "Does your partner love you?" most men responded with a high degree of certainty that they were sure of their love for their partners but less certain concerning their partner's emotions toward them. For instance, a man said, "I love her but I don't know if she loves me. I don't see any signs that she loves me because she never shows me any." Whereas in men's perception, their love toward their partners needed no proof and could be taken for granted, their partners' emotions toward them needed specific proof to be found in the women's behavior. When compared to men, women love and feel loved in a continuous and steady manner: "I love my husband a whole lot. I also feel he loves me a lot." Talking about love becomes one of the complications of living in violence, trying to overcome it, justifying it, and protecting a positive self-evaluation in the process. The man regards himself as needy (i.e., in constant need for proof of love) and his partner as a suspect who needs to bring proof of her feelings and to constantly reassure him. This enables him to balance the violence by presenting himself as a victim and to protect his self-esteem by emphasizing his altruistic and unconditional love for his partner. However, by framing his experience as being in constant suspense regarding her feelings toward him and under constant threat of losing her, he insidiously develops the moral justification for his next act of violence intended to reconquer her love. Thus, he can construct violence as an expression of love for his partner. Once we accept the idea that violence becomes a dominant factor in the couple's emotional world, the gaps in partners' perceptions of the other's emotions become catalysts of violence. In other words, if the woman reaffirms her love, she will have no cards left to negotiate with, thereby rendering herself easy prey. If she makes her love conditional, the man's sense of being threatened will be confirmed and his violence justified.

Expressions of Love

Partners' expressions of love or lack of love are an important manifestation of their joint reality. These expressions are part and parcel of all dyadic interactions. They can be represented along a continuum ranging from the fostering of love, through love-neutral expressions, to expressions that hinder love. Each partner has his or her own scale of love, which is dynamic and may change situationally. There is an ongoing negotiation toward achieving a joint scale. It will be shown that once one of the partners locates his or her emotional expression at a particular place on the scale, he or she will tend to adjust interpersonal events accordingly. Obviously, there is inherent tension in the process of negotiation, particularly when the aforementioned adjustment fails. In the following example, a batterer makes a clear distinction between various emotional expressions:

Interviewer: How do you show your wife that you love her?

Man: I don't really know how to show love. But on second thought, I would say that I have lots of feelings toward her. On specific days, specific times, I would tell her. . . . There was a time in the past she would also tell me, but at the present, she says nothing. Sometimes, I would spoil her by doing things at home, bring things home. But I think these are un-related to love. 'Cause I live in that house, I have kids in that house. If I had money, I would buy her golden jewelry and dia-monds. But I have no money. I can scream, swear, I can do all these things, but they will not have anything to do with love. Violence is just a few hours. Some short-lived grief.

This man draws the distinction between the love-fostering and love-hindering interactions. Both violence-related and love-related events are presented as clearly distinct and short-lived, whereas normal, everyday-life interactions take up most of the interpersonal time. He states that he has feelings for his partner but doesn't know how to show them. Verbal expressions are the only ones used, but they re-main scarce, limited in time and space. He considers behavioral ex-pressions of his that could be related to love as unrelated to it but as expressions of his normative obligations arising from sharing the liv-ing space with his family. Such scarce expressions are justified, from his standpoint, by his wife's complete abstention from expressing love as he experiences her. This places his partner in a symmetrical position to his on the love continuum, which in turn legitimizes his position. For instance, his "spoiling" her is presented as part of everyday inter-action rather than as love, because if it betrayed love, it would place him in an inferior position. By minimizing violence as a "short-lived grief" and by making expressions of love trivial, a balance is struck: not much love and not a lot of violence. If violence were given more volume, it is likely that love would also have been augmented.

Love is expressed either in verbal terms (e.g., "I would give her a word of praise here and there or a compliment" or "when I love him, I would tell him straight out"), or in material terms (e.g., "let's say she would need a sweat suit, and the kid would need shoes and I would need underwear, I would buy her the sweat suit first, 'cause it is impor-tant that she should be happy"), or through helping behavior (e.g., "when I feel love and she gets back from school in the evening, I prepare her a meal and even wash the dishes for her"), or emotional support (e.g., "I would ask him how he is doing, how his day was, I care about him, and that's how I express love"), or physical touch (e.g., "kisses, hugs, and sex are expressions of love"). Obviously, combinations of these expressions occur, as well as the various nuances and meanings assigned to them. There are many tactical considerations involved in choosing a specific combination. Thus, expressions of love for some partners can be perceived by others as everyday dyadic interactions. Most women express love verbally, whereas most men are incapable of it and view it as sign of superficiality and hypocrisy. Also among most couples studied, a major gap was identified between what each partner perceived as the most desirable expression of love and the way love was expressed in their actual lives. The expression of love by women was different from that by men. However, as long as there was a perceived symmetry in expression, it was considered as love. When a gap in the expression of love was discerned by one of the partners, it was translated into loss of love.

The inductive categories of love and expression of love emerging from our interview material can be organized along two axes: One is related to the correspondence between the expectations and expressions of love of both partners. This axis ranges from complete correspondence to total lack of correspondence. The second axis is related to the continuum of expressing love, ranging from fostering to hindering love.

Figure 5.1 is a graphic representation of four extreme options arising from the interaction between these axes:

1. Expression of love is fostered, and there is a high degree of correspondence between the partners in expectations and expression. In this case, there is marital satisfaction, partners are secure, and they live in a mutually satisfying relationship. The likelihood of violence in such cases is low.

2. Expressions of love are fostered, but there is little correspondence between the partners in expectations and expressions. The likelihood of dissatisfaction within the couple is high, as at least one party will experience unreciprocated love (i.e., the relationship is asymmetrical). This is an untenable situation over time and is a subliminal expectation that something must change in either expression or expectation so correspondence may be reestablished.

3. Expressions of love are hindered, and there is a low level of correspondence between expectations and actual love-related behav-

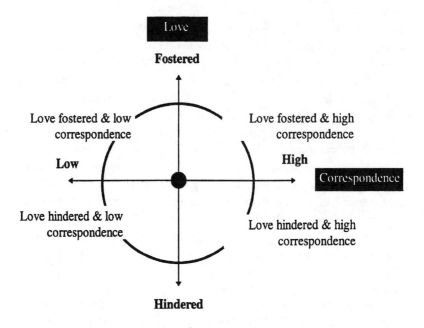

Figure 5.1. Expressions and Correspondence in Love

iors. This leads to attempts to either increase the expressions or to reinstate correspondence. But if these attempts fail, the likelihood for violence is high. Violence is an extreme attempt to reestablish the balance in the relationship, and as such, it does comprise a peculiar element of hope.

4. Expressions of love are hindered, and there is high correspondence between lack of expectations and lack of expression. In this case, violence is probable, and partners are likely to come to terms with it and perceive it as part of their dyadic routine. Thus, there is little hope that anything will change in the relationship.

Locating Violence in the Context of Love

Partners need to find ways to live day to day with violence. So they either integrate love with violence, or they separate them completely. When violence is incorporated, several combined arguments are suggested by the partners to make the point that violence is functional to the relationship. These can be ranged along a continuum, with one end maintaining that although violence and love are essentially different, their combination can be helpful to the relationship; the other-end arguments purport to equate love and violence and blur the boundaries between the two. For instance, a man said,

> Perhaps, it distances us [violence], but it also brings us closer. Because look, there is no such thing that partners wouldn't argue. There are no such couples. 'Cause when you argue, you hate, but you also love . . . and whoever argues more and hates more, he also loves more. In the final analysis, these things [violence] bring you closer.

The use of spatial terms indicates that to the speaker, violence affects both closeness and distance but ultimately leads to proximity. This man also equates love and hate at the level of the intensity of the emotions: By both being intense, they are experienced as identical. Moreover, a functional relationship is presented as obtaining between the two emotions: The more violence, the more love. Cessation of violence, then, is tantamount to cessation of love. Once the fusion is established and the inseparability of violence from love is made explicit, one can speak about the one emotion in terms of the other: Violence and love become synonymous and can be contrasted with other feelings, such as indifference. As one man put it,

> Violence is an expression of love. Actually, it shows that the feeling we feel towards each other is strong. It's exactly the opposite of indifference. Love is also the opposite of indifference. So it turns out that they are the same, not the opposite. . . . I know there are people who think differently about this.

Another woman carried the functional argument one step further: "The violence strengthens our love. . . .'Cause when it is all over, after all, it brings us to look more in depth at why and what keeps us together." Here, violence is presented as strengthening the relationship by allowing the partners to examine their togetherness with the violence in the background. As such, it provides depth and perspective, enabling the reorganization and thus fortification of the relationship.

When love is disrupted by violence, the two must be effectively kept apart to enable living with both. Thus, specific means of separation can be discerned. One is related to drawing a qualitative distinction between love and violence and presenting them as diametrical opposites: One is contaminated, the other is pure; one is bad, the other is good, and so forth. To achieve this, a tactic of fragmentation is employed. The following quote by a woman illustrates this:

> We had many violent episodes in our life. These events were real disgusting. I am not trying to say they were OK, but our general feeling is that violence and love don't belong to each other. But all in all, this [violence] doesn't belong to love. It didn't influence the love. At least as far as I am concerned, it did not. It didn't change a thing.

Another means of achieving insulation is to minimize violence by manipulating it in time and memory. A woman said, "Yes, violence does have an influence but only while we are actually fighting. Not beyond that. After that, I forget it as if nothing happened, and I continue loving him." By restricting the duration of the impact of violence and by moving it in memory to a place where it can be forgotten, violence is denied. We can say then that when violence and love are perceived as mutually exclusive or contradictory, violence needs to be denied for love to continue.

Guilt

When the previously described emotional balance between partners is tipped, someone must take responsibility for the escalation, as a first step toward reestablishing the balance. Our contention is that a precondition for the assumption of responsibility is a feeling of guilt. The following quote from the words of a battered woman illustrates the power of guilt:

> After violence, there is a lot of guilt. I don't know how I express it outwardly, but inside, I am paralyzed. Sort of obtuse. Here is how it goes: I am either real angry and in an uncontrolled outburst, or I am in this sort of withdrawal and out of touch with myself. As if I am trying to hide away from myself. It's a situation in which it is difficult to look at myself and observe my own behavior.

Because guilt is experienced as a painful experience, the battered woman is trying to minimize the impact of situations that are guilt inducing: "I am trying to do things which will keep me away from guilt. I am not leaving the house, I have no friends, nothing. So God forbid, I wouldn't feel I did something bad." When guilt is prevalent among couples living in violence, the needed step toward assuming responsibility cannot be taken for granted. Partners can experience

guilt and be stuck in it without assuming responsibility for the violence. One way of doing this is to experience guilt or lack of guilt in
inverted proportion to the partner: "If I feel guilty, he doesn't; and if
he feels guilty, I won't." The other way is to disconnect behaviors
from their guilt-producing consequences: "He said to me, you are
guilty. When he's guilty, I am guilty; when I am guilty, obviously I am
also guilty. I am guilty in any case." The third is to use guilt as a rationale for violence:

> Always, but always, she's guilty. And she feels guilty. . . . But for her
> to recognize it, I have to force it. To use force. It never happened that
> she would come to me and say, "Listen, I am guilty."

Last, one can use guilt to cause suffering to the partner, in response to
violence and to get even: "I love to make him feel bad. I know I have
some guilt, too, but I love to make him suffer. And I put all the blame
on him." The violence may be seen as a way to lay responsibility on the
partner and regain what is perceived as lost by the refusal to assume it.
However, once responsibility is assumed by one partner, it becomes
clear that no one knows what has been lost. Hence, the question,
"Responsibility for what?" remains unanswered, and the recurrence
of violence is inevitable. Once violence takes place, it becomes the
only concrete, palpable issue for negotiation and by focusing on violence, responsibility, which is basically ephemeral, is sidestepped.
Without addressing the responsibility issue, there is no way to redress
the balance. This keeps the partners in a continuous deadlock. At
some point, an agreement is reached or enforced concerning the
responsibility for the violence. This accord is generalized to the entire
issue of responsibility and brings the couple to a sense of virtual balance. However, the balance is unreal, fragile, and cannot hold for
long. Thus, violence is likely to become a routine avenue for negotiating virtual responsibility.

So long as partners have not arrived at an agreement concerning
blame and responsibility, the circle of violence is likely to continue. In
such cases, each partner feels that he or she was doubly wronged: In
the perpetrator's subjective experience, he feels that he was denied
love and is expected to take responsibility for it. The victim experiences that she was physically abused and that she is expected to be
responsible for the abuse. Such situations are unbearable, and one of
the partners is likely to find a way to back off or to be forced to do
so. This is a temporary state, as partners cannot live with the
experience of being doubly wronged for long. Thus, each explicitly

demands that the other feel guilty and take responsibility. Taking responsibility is a relief for both partners and a precondition for reinstating the balance in their relationship. They tend to distinguish between guilt, which is perceived as the deserved punishment of the one who is blamed, and responsibility, which is felt to be the compensation of the offended party. Guilt is perceived as more difficult to bear and to understand, for it is a much more profound experience. One can assume responsibility and not feel guilty, but it is more difficult to assume guilt without feeling responsible. For instance, one can distance himself or herself from responsibility, once he or she acknowledges it on the declarative level, without experiencing guilt. On the other hand, one cannot distance oneself from feeling guilty once one experiences it. This distinction implies that conflicts can be solved by taking responsibility without feeling guilty. When both are demanded by one of the parties, an unbearable situation ensues, which usually leads to an escalation. The negotiation is no longer over guilt and responsibility but rather over punishment and compensation.

Expressions of Responsibility and Compensation

Once the partners come to an agreement concerning responsibility for the violence, the responsible party is expected to express his or her recognition behaviorally. This is done by a variety of compensating strategies, ranging in intensity from overcompensation to hardly visible attempts to compensate.

When compensation is intense, it is often difficult to distinguish it from expressions of love, as described earlier. For instance, one man said,

> After the violence, I am real gentle, I am trying to make up for the fact that I bursted out and lost it. And after several days, in which I am expressing more love than usual, this dissipates, and we go back to the regular love, which is somewhere in between violence and great love.

This quote illustrates that the man takes responsibility for the violence and attempts to compensate his partner by a "dose" of love which he alone defines as appropriate in terms of intensity and duration. His measuring is reflected in the expression, "real gentleness." Once the special dose is administered, things can go back to some routine level of love, which he distinguishes from great love, again by criteria that he alone decides on. He locates this normative level between violence and what he calls great love. Now, he can stop being "real gentle" and go back to his usual self. The partner has been compensated and is expected to get over the violence. Women expressed a similar construct concerning responsibility and compensation. One woman said,

> After we make up, and we start talking, yes. . . . I feel he regrets the whole thing and is trying to get closer, touch, I feel he loves me more. We both feel the love is returning between us. At such times, it is real intense, but then it gets back to normal.

This quote shows that expressions of regret by the partner come to substitute for total estrangement. Communicating and touching signal the resumption of contact following the assumption of responsibility. His regrets are the beginning of the dialogue, rapprochement, and expressions of love. The use of the "we" pronoun signals acknowledgment by the woman of their renewed togetherness. His gestures of compensation bring the lost love back. The readiness for this stage is highlighted by the unbearable tension involved in being distanced over time. A man described this as follows:

> What we have here is one stubborn woman. Perhaps, I would define the situation as "who will blink first." I must recognize that I have difficulties to express feelings, but I can't tell what would be her reaction. Perhaps, she'll reject me, perhaps she'll be pissed. . . . So in general, I am hesitant. There are times when after [the violence], she would lie in bed by me, wouldn't sleep, expects that I hug her, that I calm her down. And I am waiting myself . . .'cause she needs to give something, a sign of life. So what if I am the man. And it turns out that we do nothing, and we are both frustrated.

From this description, we learn that when partners are distanced following violence, they are walking the edge and expecting each other to yield. The man attributes his inability to back off first to his emotional setup. He further describes the risks in yielding first as related to his partner's unpredictable reactions. He believes she is stubborn, and he cannot take the risk of a rejection. Thus, they position themselves in a waiting mode, filled with tension and expectation. Taking responsibility will relieve the tension but will also mean that he blinked first.

We have shown that the partners' emotional experience unfolds in several stages: There is a nonviolent routine with regular expressions of love; there is a conflict followed by violence in which love dissipates; there is a stage of distancing and estrangement; a stage of assuming responsibility driven by guilt and expressed by enhanced manifestations of love; and last, a return to the routine. The last two stages mentioned already contain the seeds of the next conflict for two reasons. First, the enhanced manifestations of love raise the expectations on the everyday level. One cannot go back to previous routines, because they are experienced as inferior in the light of the intensive emotional experiences during compensation. Second, once partners return to an emotional routine, the stage of intense emotions is reframed as fake, unreal. The compensation was achieved by deception. Partners who felt doubly wronged add now a third layer to their sense of disillusionment, that of being deceived.

Another small group of perpetrators of violence do little if anything to manifest responsibility for the violent acts. For this group, the guilt or the assumption of responsibility is a nonissue. Because violence is denied, one feels neither guilty nor responsible for it, and thus there is no need to find ways of compensation. For example, a woman said,

> When my husband is angry, he can be violent. But soon after, he feels nothing particularly different. As far as he is concerned, his wife can be nearby, sleep by his side, and he has no problem with it whatsoever. He can fight with me, and a half an hour later, he can tell me, "How are you, honey? How are you feeling?" . . . At the time of the argument, he can be upset, but he can close it up and behave as if nothing happened.

From the woman's view point, her partner denies the violence, and he successfully brackets out from his experience the need for compensation. For him, life is continuous in its routine in spite of the occurrence of violence. Such bracketing, however, leaves the partner frustrated and angry.

Summary

In this chapter, we chose to focus on two emotions: love and guilt. Although these are by no means the only emotions involved in intimate violence, we believe they are powerful markers of violent events. Love as well as guilt can be either a buffer or a catalyst of violence. The temporal unfolding of these emotions and violence is significant in understanding the partners' emotional experience. Love precedes violence, whereas guilt is viewed as a consequence of it. From such sequencing, we learn that paradoxically, love is perceived by partners as generating violence (through the experience of its loss), and guilt is viewed as enabling partners to seek and generate renewed love. From their perspective, violence becomes a regulator of love and guilt. Responsibility helps to delineate the boundaries of the relationship and subsequent expectations and as such, generates both. It can be said that once this sequence becomes routinized in the couple's everyday life, violence is transformed from a regulator to a complex emotion and container, modulating all other emotions. Couples living in violence move from a situation in which emotions and violence live side by side to a situation in which emotions and violence are one. This fusion becomes the background coloring of their entire experience.

6

The Metaphoric
Understanding
of Violence

Because it is through language that we enter the world of couples living in violence, it may come as no surprise if we find that, in correspondence to the two irreducibly different points of view on the violent event itself, there will be two different languages, the language of the batteringman and that of his battered wife. And indeed, our considerable database of interviews points clearly to a qualitative difference between the languages used by the different genders. The crucial difference lies in what may be termed a set of *constitutive metaphors*.

It turns out that in describing his life in violence, the man invariably deploys war images, whereas his wife uses control imagery. That is to say, in the batterer's narrative (as a whole), there is a leading metaphor that constitutes his inner world, the one he shares with his wife in violence. This leading metaphor colors his language to the extent that it appears different from his wife's language, which is dominated by her leading metaphor.

In this chapter, we explore these constitutive metaphors. Obviously, these metaphors occur in narratives recounted by two parties who have completely different roles in the situation. What can we learn from this correspondence between language and behavior?

The Metaphoric World of Batterers

Two broad thematic areas have been identified among batterers' metaphors: One is related to conflict and violence expressed and constructed in war metaphors; the other has to do with metaphors presenting the self as a dangerous space and as a locus of inner struggles. The former are both descriptive and constitutive of an all-encompassing life context; the latter are more focused on the self.

Conflict and Violence Expressed in War Metaphors

War metaphors are central to men's descriptions of conflicts with their partners. The metaphorical depiction of the conflict as a war effects a qualitative change in the overall perception of the relationship by the man. For instance, a man who was asked to describe the escalation from conflict to violence said, "How does it happen? This is a war. Everyone is trying to fight his own battles." This metaphorical representation enables him to present a balanced picture: There are no victims and perpetrators; each party is as active and as responsible as the other. The definition of conflicts as wars connotes intensity, destruction, and unpredictability. The situation becomes charged and escalatory. There is a danger of loss of control to the point of chaos. A batterer described the escalation as follows: "Everyone is digging in. Each in his own position. No one is willing to give in. There is no way out." The conflict is visualized here as trench warfare, a war of attrition without foreseeable breakthroughs or retreats. The metaphor also encapsulates the chronic nature of the conflict. There is no end to the war. The use of impersonal language as a strategy of distancing is noteworthy: "everyone" is digging in; "no one is willing"; "each one" is in his own position. Such usage also generalizes the predicament. In addition, through it, the man draws a picture of his loneliness in a hostile environment. He is alone in the trenches.

Even if the man is focused on himself and aware of his actions, the metaphor of war forces him to concentrate on the other as a source of danger. A man said,

> In cases when she was hitting me back, I started feeling it [the anger] . . . in my head, in my hands, eyes. . . . Instead of cooling it, I start heating up . . till I burst up in one shot. She cries and gets upset, she wants to run me over, but she stops herself and cries again.

The man here is aware of the process of getting angry and becoming violent. He describes it in a metaphor of rising temperature: "heating up." This is an escalatory metaphor. The mechanism fuels itself. Because it will not stop itself, it must explode as the only way to end. The man's self-awareness is trapped in the metaphor of inevitability and escalation. The woman's reaction is also perceived in the same metaphoric context. She cries, gets upset, and is thus expected to be getting ready to attack. Even if she stops and cries, these attempts are remembered in the context of a script in which her behaviors are precursors of retaliation. The man perceives her reaction as similar to his way of reacting, so it is familiar and can be kept within the same metaphoric framework.

Once the other is identified as a source of danger, the way to overcome it is by being more dangerous than the other. This becomes evident in depicting the home as an arena for interpersonal power struggles: "She knows where all my soft spots are. She also knows that when she hits me, I throw up my hands. But believe me, I know her soft spots, too."

The implicit tactics employed here are the hiding of weaknesses on the one hand and using cunning and surprise on the other. One will also note that the language of this metaphor is close and personal, in keeping with the close physical contact characteristic of wrestling. The man presents his partner as the initiator and himself as reacting passively. By furthermore presenting the partner as keenly aware of his weak spots, he attributes intellectual capabilities to her that are superior to his and against which he needs to defend himself.

When the partner is seen as the enemy who is going for the other's weak spots, intimacy becomes dangerous. Fear and threat emerge as a central theme in battering men's perceptions of their lives with their partners. The man purposefully places his ability to hurt the other and his own vulnerability at the center of the intimate relationship. This has threatening power in and of itself. When the female partner in the relationship knows that the other can and will hurt her, she needs to take this into account in every aspect of the relationship, not only when the threat is immediate and imminent. Men describe their violence as a natural reaction to women's attempts to hit them in their weak spots. One batterer described his violence metaphorically as follows: "When I saw she had discovered my weakness, I was forced to defend myself. I had to be strong to defend myself. So I went at her." When the man feels caught in his weakness, the distinction in his perception between attack and defense becomes blurred. In this context, men often use the metaphor of retreat: "Today, once more, we are faced with a deteriorating situation. All I do is try to absorb the shocks and slow her down. Things have been deteriorating between us again since I retreated." As in wars, where the loss of one battle encourages the enemy to attack again, here, too, the man perceives his partner as increasing her aggression because of his retreat. This places the conflict on an escalatory course with a predictable direction.

The next metaphor locates the conflict in the legal sphere. Here again, the violent man perceives himself as losing the battle: "You ask the questions, you answer them; you are the judge and the prosecutor. Is there anything left for me to say? No matter what, I am always the defendant." This brings the man's perception of powerlessness in the war against his partner to a climax. He now views himself as a victim of injustice, too, the victim of a systematic conspiracy of which his partner is only one party. Violent men end up believing that their violence is reactive to the violent framework created by their partners, which leaves them with no way out. The following quote is illustrative:

> The minute a woman allows herself to swear or to hit, there is a boundary which I will not let her invade. In the argument, you get to a point that you keep talking and you see suddenly that the other person reacts with her hands. You get to a point that you see that without hands, it will not help. You move on to the other person's method, you only understand his method.

The partner is perceived as a person who needs to be forced to behave within certain constraints. If the woman transcends the bounds of her gender role, as he sees it, he will inevitably react appropriately. The man circumscribes boundaries that define his territorial claims. An invasion of his space is defined as "casus belli." When the woman behaves contrarily to her gender role expectations, she is masculinized and depersonalized in one fell swoop. She becomes the "other person" who is as powerful as the man and dangerous enough to warrant violent action. Violence is not the man's method but hers; she has invaded the space, moved beyond her boundaries; thus, she'll be punished.

All these imaginary forces and frames help the man to preserve his good self-image and avoid self-definition as an aggressor. At the same time, he knows that he is violent. Thus, the only way to settle this contradiction is to define himself as a "battering victim." The metaphors of war enable the man to define his violence as self-defense and the war as justified, thus eliciting public approval for his actions and

defending his positive public image. In war, as men define it metaphorically, only two mutually exclusive solutions are possible: victory
or defeat. Every conflict is a battle, and every battle affects the final
outcome of the war. When situations are defined in such a dramatic
and dichotomous fashion, violence is called for.

Through war metaphors, violent men gradually construct a reality
in which their violence is imposed on them by their partners. In such a
newly created reality, the man perceives himself as a novice and an
apprentice, his previous life experiences with his partner are becoming irrelevant, and he realizes that he will have to acquire a whole new
set of skills, thinking habits, and behaviors, which are essential in his
war for survival. Because he defines the interpersonal situation as war,
he assumes the identity of a soldier. The violence that was accounted
for in terms of war becomes the warrior's way of life.

Metaphors Representing Inner Space as
Dangerous and a Locus of Inner Struggles

Many batterers use metaphors that focus on the body and on
forces acting within the body to express conflicts and violence. The
body is a major source of orientation of the self in one's life space. People use it as a principal point of reference for receiving and sending
messages. The body is the boundary between the individual's inner
and outer space. As such, it is a major component of one's sense of
security. Metaphors men use to refer to their inner space express their
perception of themselves and others and the extent to which they feel
a loss of control, cognitively and emotionally, when this inner space is
invaded. One violent man described the ways in which the anger he
views as coming from the outside enters the body and is held within:

> Arguments and arguments again. "Why did you come late? Where
> were you? What did you do?" How long can one take this? Day after
> day. Five times a day. It piles up and it tears your body apart. It leaves
> no place for you. . . . I really don't want to fight. . . . I hear the edgy
> words, shut up, and swallow.

Metaphors of eating and swallowing are illustrative of the ways men
view the way they handle arguments. These quarrels are perceived as
something that penetrates their bodies, as though they were force-fed.
Underlying the metaphor of being force-fed is a loss of control over
what they take in. The forced input is what takes over. A man used the
metaphor of a balloon that blows up to emphasize the idea:

> At home, you live from one minute to the other. I often feel like a
> balloon: You blow in it, and blow in it, and blow in it again. As it
> grows and grows, it changes. You don't remember how it used to be
> anymore. And then, the situation is that there is no more room for
> the last blow and it blows up.

Events take place on a predictable time arrow: His balloon will never
let air out, it keeps blowing fuller and fuller, it changes shape and size,
to the point of explosion. The man as balloon is flexible and passive.
He keeps adjusting to the content placed in him by the woman. Once
blown beyond its capacity, he—the balloon—explodes, and as such,
it cannot contain anymore. The expectation of danger is constructed
on the basis of the idea of overextension by a force that does not depend on the man. Moreover, the man is now in a position were he
rightfully regards any so-called blow as a deliberate attempt to make
the balloon explode. His situation is dangerous, and any provocation
by the woman is now weightier by far. This metaphor of the explosion
of the balloon has a double meaning in the man's experience: It serves
to account for his violent outbursts, but it also expresses his concern
for his physical integrity.

Needless to say, these two meanings interact in creating a switch
between the roles of the perpetrator and the victim. The aggressor is
now the woman, who violates the man's inner space in spite of his best
efforts to contain her. The man has constructed a reality composed of
contradictory demands: not to be violent but also, to avoid being a victim, and thus he feels trapped in the way he handles anger. Letting it
out is dangerous; keeping it in is harmful. This forces him to attempt
to detach himself from his emotions. The man and his anger are at
odds: "I don't hold it inside. If something hurts me, I get it out. I
explode. I will not let it stay in my body." Or similarly, "Anger, anger
. . . if I keep it in it's bad. I have to think how to get it out." The man
has no solution for his anger. Whatever he does with his anger, it will
turn against him. Getting one's anger out can lead to unforeseeable
consequences: "Sometimes, I get my anger out and then want to leave.
I blame myself. Perhaps I should leave and give her a break." Contradictory demands generate conflicting emotions: Whereas being a perpetrator is associated with anger, becoming a victim generates guilt.
The fantasy of leaving may alleviate the tension. But he will never
leave because it is unrelated to the situation that triggered it. It rather
springs from the man's need to solve the unbearable tension created by
contradictory emotions. Leaving is not "giving her a break" but rather
giving himself one. At the same time, the statement about the willing-

ness to leave to give her a break is subliminally designed to present himself as a responsible person who is willing to sacrifice for the sake of protecting his partner's well-being. Thus, the perpetrator will enter the next violent situation from a position of moral superiority. In any event, he realizes that his thermodynamic "solution" for releasing pressure creates more pressure but this time, on his partner rather than on himself.

The men realize that the process is Sisyphean and circular in nature. Whatever avenues they choose, violent men are at war either externally (e.g., angry) or internally (e.g., guilty). By trying to reduce inner tension and pass it on to their partners, they create an ever-growing state of tension and turmoil in their intimate lives:

> I regret it, anyway. In spite of what I said, in spite of the fact that she deserves it, I feel bad about my behavior, about what I did to her. I think it all over, and it accumulates all over again. Every argument with its own leftover.

This quote illustrates how the cumulative effect of violent events in intimate relationships leads to an increasing shift in the experience of the perpetrators from focusing on the relationship to focusing on oneself. This perception is expressed through internal conflicts. There is a sense of an increasing rift between one part that is identified with the violent self and another that is trying to overpower it:

> When I hit her, I felt I was blowing apart. It's something coming from inside, you cannot stop. I contain myself a lot. You don't know how much. I can give her a small slap, and she can fall down. Because of this, I am careful with myself. I am holding myself. I am guarding myself. I am trying to overcome myself.

The means by which the man attempts to control the violent self are also violent. As in a civil war, the self is divided. The hectic attempts to control, conquer, and overcome the self underline a lack of self-trust (what else is this self capable of?). The less one trusts one's self, the more one needs to use force to control it. Thus, the man is caught up in a spiraling process of splitting, using the nonviolent part of the self to control the violent part. To achieve this goal, force is needed. When successful in avoiding violence toward his partner, the man is violent toward himself; when he fails, the violence is directed toward his partner.

The metaphors of war through which batterers describe their world are interconnected. They are fighting on internal as well as external battlefields. When the outside world is regarded as dangerous, any retreat is seen as life-threatening, as in a war. Thus, for a man who regards himself as helpless, threatening with violence is to defend the self (i.e., literally, self-defense). By perceiving their violence through war metaphors, the batterers render their actions meaningful in a peculiar way. The paradox inherent in defining attack as defense, defense as loss, and loss as surrender is that by using such extreme and exclusionary definitions, men unwittingly preserve their experience of weakness as the basis for current and future violence. The only way to overcome one's weakness is through violence. The only way to defend one's self is by hurting others. Self-control is achieved through loss of control.

Metaphors used to describe violent acts and their resolution are a thorough representation of the complexity of the violence. On the one hand, metaphors of war connote chaos, impulsiveness, and complete loss of control; on the other hand, they impose a framework suggesting much predetermination, reflective planning, and strategizing. This leaves the men with both options open in their presentation of self to the world; they see themselves as living in a framed chaos in which they can still weigh options and make choices. Thus, they can present themselves as either premeditative or impulsive, or even as both at the same time, as the situation demands.

Because the data for our book were collected and interpreted in Israel, a country at war since its foundation, one could suppose that the use of war metaphors is culturally specific. However, it appears to us that these findings are gender rather than culture specific. A metaphoric perception of life as war reflects the "warrior psyche" of manhood in general (Keen, 1992). This perception is centered on an attitude toward life situations that views conflicts as an intensive struggle between good and bad, hero and villain, victory and defeat. This dichotomous and polar perception is colored by intense and opposite emotions, such as love and hate, loyalty and betrayal, courage and cowardice. The world is black and white, and life is a constant struggle against actual and imagined enemies. To survive in a reality constructed by such metaphors, one has to suppress feelings such as weakness, fear, compassion, and guilt, and degrade the feminine as epitomizing all weakness. The batterer is a gender warrior whose failed macho complex is always threatening him (Gondolf & Hanneken, 1987).

The Metaphoric World
of Battered Women

The metaphoric world of battered women centers on the theme of coping with control-related issues. The metaphoric expressions of control can be divided into two themes: one of gaining and the other of losing control.

Gaining Control

Attempts to gain control are related to drawing the boundaries between violence and nonviolence, predicting the occurrence of violence, and managing it when it occurs.

Mapping the Metaphoric
Boundaries of Violence

In battered women's experience, living in violence necessitates a degree of orientation regarding their interpersonal situations and the positions of their partners in them. To achieve this, women need to place boundaries between violent and nonviolent situations as well as to be able to characterize violent situations and the actors involved in them. To this end, women clearly distinguish between situations in which their male partners are violent and those in which they are not. Within these boundaries, several experiential typologies are created. For instance, one woman stated, "He never hits when he is not angry. When he's angry, he can't control his nerves, and he lifts his hands. He can't control himself, simply can't control himself. When his anger goes beyond his capacity, violence is coming." In this quote, the woman identifies the coming violence by the man's capacity to handle his anger. The capacity metaphor signals the boundaries of responsibility: He is in charge until he reaches his full capacity, and she needs to take over beyond that point. Such an approach goes beyond creating boundaries in that mutual expectations are formed concerning responsibility. By so doing, the woman constructs a situation in which she either succeeds in keeping the partner's anger within his capacities, or else she becomes victimized by her own failure. Although this construct may sound absurd at first, it does have several important functions: First, it sets limits to the man's violence and as such, it makes it bearable; second, it makes violence familiar and controllable; third, it gives the woman a sense of control over the development of the violence. Thus, she can transform herself from a passive victim into a manager of her own victimization.

Another woman stresses her partner's loss of control in accounting for his denial of responsibility: "He tells me he doesn't control himself since he didn't expect it coming. Actually, when he calms down, he feels he didn't want to get to that point." This brief quote expresses two major components of the previous construct: One is the relating of violence to the partner's loss of control and the other expresses regret concerning the consequences of his loss of control. The woman can reconstruct her violent partner metaphorically into a helpless and innocent person who places himself at her mercy. Such "humble surrender" can easily be taken as an expression of affection and love. She is now both fully responsible and expected to accept and return love. From that point on, any violence is a sign that she failed to reciprocate his love.

Metaphors of control describe both situational and processual dimensions of relationships permeated by violence. To describe the processual aspects, battered women use spatiotemporal metaphors. One such metaphor is "loss of way." The following quote is instructive: "Everything is on its path until he suddenly flips, and he doesn't know where he's taking us. When this happens, I get lost with him." The relationship is going in a definite direction until violence occurs; direction is temporarily lost for the duration of the violence and subsequently, one gets back on track. This way, violence can be understood both as an accident, an isolated occurrence, and as a temporary derailment from a track that is usually nonviolent. By such metaphorical tactics, women can live with a sustained sense of control of the so-called beaten path and bracket out the derailings as nonrepresentative occurrences. A woman said, "I hesitate to talk, and believe me, I am no coward; 'cause he gets into this amok and he loses direction. He gave me a swollen face. When he is into this amok, he has no control over himself." Another woman described her partner's violence as follows: "From within his nerves, he can't see what's going on at that specific moment, what comes out of him. The minute he's agitated, everything comes out of him." This quote presents a sharp distinction between inner and outer space. In the woman's perception, inner space is associated with control. Violence expressed out of agitation signals a leak, from inside outward. Because the man is upset, he ceases to be part of what is going on. He is unaware of his leak and of the specific moment it occurs. Once things begin to come out, they are uncontrolled, and the leak becomes a torrent: "Everything comes out of him."

Predicting Violence

Two polar situations have been identified in our interviews concerning predictability: one in which women can predict the imminence of violence, the other in which they cannot and therefore need to account for it. The woman in the following quote cannot predict the violence of her partner. She said,

> I am always taken by surprise at first. . . . In spite of the fact that I am well aware of the problem. . . . It bursts out like a rocket. . . . You can never understand why and how things get out of control."

The woman in this quote "predicts" the unpredictability of the violence. That is, although the details surrounding it are unpredictable, the very outburst is known, familiar, and expected. Because neither the woman nor the man have control over the timing, there is a sense of loss of control. Anger with a rocketlike strength is quite forgivably beyond the man's control. This in turn legitimizes the woman's loss of control. When the situation is out of control, the violence is depersonalized. "It" is out of control. By so doing, the woman achieves a successful distinction between not being able to control the violence and her inability to control her partner's violence. She is thus able to lose control of the violence while keeping familiarity and knowledge of her partner.

A recurring theme in the interviews we analyzed was that when prediction became problematic, some sort of split was always attempted by battered women. In the previous section, we showed how women isolate the violence from their partners. The metaphoric perception of the partner enables the woman to create another kind of differentiation between the violent man who attacks her and the person she chooses to live with. Two complementary facets are presented in the woman's metaphoric world. One is the partner who is transformed by violence into a stranger: "He looses control; he becomes a complete stranger . . . not the way I know him. I see something in his eyes: some meanness, sort of a scary expression on his face." By making the man out to be a stranger, the woman distances herself from him. She does not know him and his violence. Thus, she is able to set herself at a tolerable distance from his violent self and his actions and handle them with a rationality that would otherwise be impossible. On the other hand, of course, she knows him because she knows who loses control and who becomes a stranger. By distancing him, she is able to "contain" him, and by estranging herself, she becomes closer to him. By metaphorically arriving at these understandings, the woman enhances her sense of control over the violent situation without having to give up on her partner. The other facet of the same split underscores the partner's "good" image attacked by violence as a force external to him. An example is given by a woman whose partner forces her to have sex with him:

> If a person would hit . . . this is no abuse compared to what he does to me [forced sex]. This is humiliation, simply humiliation. This is in essence all the arguments we have. He, from his perception, is a nice guy . . . he has a golden heart, he's willing to give from himself a lot. But he is capricious. And it's impossible to handle this, it's impossible.

Another woman says,

> I feel pain, physical and emotional. . . . But I know him. I know he gets upset and loses it, but I know deep inside, he doesn't think about what he's doing and his intentions are good . . . only good. He can raise hands without thinking . . . but when he cools down, he returns to himself.

Violence could not destroy the woman's image and belief that the man is basically good. The physical pain and humiliation cannot ruin her need to see him that way. So to attain this goal, she separates his "golden heart" from the rest of him and makes it into the "real" truth, great enough to overshadow marital rape and the negative feelings associated with it. In the second quote, the woman attributes the man's violence to a trip outside himself. When "he returns," he finds his real self and herself waiting for him . . . together.

Other women were able to predict their partner's violence: "I started feeling his high tones, and I am very familiar with that top of his voice . . . when he looses control." To be able to control violence, it is essential to predict when it will happen and to manage it when it does. To do so, the woman has to position herself as an insider in the development of the violent events. For instance, a woman said, "There must be a fight between us to make this tension explode. He can't control his nerves, I know when he is calm and when is the time he flips; 'cause when he flips, he flips." The "I know" emphasizes the predictability of the process and the "fight between us" emphasizes her partnership in the process. It can be said that the experience of being able to manage violence will depend on the ability to reconstruct it in terms of predictability and partnership. The need for managing violence thus becomes the major concern for the battered woman.

Managing Violence

As used in this chapter, *managing violence* refers to the ability of the battered woman to manipulate the violent situation in her life and make it controllable and livable. Once the woman constructs a reality in which she can manage the violence, any specific violent event will be assessed in terms of managing successes or failures. A managing failure will motivate her to improve her managing skills rather than leave. The major tools used in managing are words. Thus, mastering the words, skill at deciding which to use and when and how, constitutes her strength. Women gradually realize that their words have the power to either control or trigger the violence. It must be said that controlling the violence presupposes its existence. We found in our interviews as well as in clinical contexts that in battered women's experience, managing is based on the taken-for-grantedness of the violence and not on its eradication. Women gradually achieve expertise in managing. This may be at the level of intuitively recognizing the power of words and may culminate in the ability to use words to control violence. The following quotes illustrate various levels of mastering the violence through talk. In the first quote, the woman knows intuitively the potential of words:

> At that moment . . . he was upset, from work. In these cases, it is enough to give him one word to light him up. . . . He simply felt he needs to blow up. To raise his hands and blow up. . . . I usually talk quietly. . . . I am trying to find out. I keep away from sensitive points. . . . I don't know why it lights him up and what happens to him, but I feel it will happen.

In this quote, the man comes home from work in an explosive mood. The woman understands intuitively that she is dealing with a highly dangerous situation for both of them and that the way she will handle it will determine the outcome. Although she has no specific knowledge of how to handle it, she does know that it requires much sensitivity and prudence.

In this next quote, a woman describes her understanding that her verbal power matches the partner's physical strength. There is a balancing act here: He hits dangerously and she talks dangerously:

> When we fight, when I have no control over my mouth, I bring things to real stormy fights. Today, I understand that he would feel really humiliated from the fact that I keep answering him, offend

him, swear at him. But it gave me some strength to do that since I had
no physical power against him.

Where the previous woman rendered the violence contingent on some
contextual variables outside her control (e.g., he came home upset
from work), this woman creates a linear, causal relationship between
her mouth and a stormy fight. She further underscores the gradual
aspect in learning how to mange violence ("Today, I understand . . .)
but only up to a certain degree: She can make him explode whenever
she likes, and she thereby gets even with him even before he acts violently. We may assume that the next step in the managing process
should be learning to control his explosions. The following quote
illustrates a higher degree of managing, as the woman recognizes the
power of words not only in the creation of violence but also in controlling it:

> At times, the man has no control over himself and raises his hands.
> Men are really more nervous than women. You can talk him into cra-
> ziness. He can shut up, shut up and not stop. And he than loses con-
> trol. It depends what words you use with him.

This description is patently saturated with gender consciousness: The
silent man can hold in his rage, but he can't talk; and the woman who
can, talks him into anything she likes. She can prod a passive man to
violence or not, she has the choice of where she wants to lead him to.
She controls the situation by controlling the words. Furthermore, as
she constructs a metaphorical reality of control through words, she
must also reassess the power of silence in this reality. She is bound to
attribute great might to the man's silence, and she knows that his way
of controlling her is by silence. Thus, when she decides to "shut up,"
she successfully reframes this as a source of control. By so doing,
silence becomes a sign of strength and control over the situation rather
than a sign of capitulation and humiliation. The man is like a walking
bomb constantly threatening to go off. The woman feels that it is up to
her to defuse the bomb and thereby control the situation through
silence.

Losing Control

So far, we have attempted to show how women who live with
their violent partners construct their joint lives as a controllable reality
and the benefits they derive from the meaning structure they build.

However, not all women are able to achieve such meaning, because to do so, at least two preconditions have to be satisfied: One is that their partners cooperate with their construction of control and the other is that they have the managing abilities to develop and maintain this construct. When this is not the case, most of their energy goes into controlling the damage arising from the loss of control. The following quotes are illustrative:

> When he's pissed, I know immediately he is about to lose control. I am trying real hard to be silent in these situations in order to avoid his getting out of control. . . . I never understood what is he jealous of. I am locking myself totally. . . . As if someone placed a lock on my entire body. At these moments, I am frightened. I prefer to put locks on my mouth and not to say a word. . . . I simply force myself into control. I am about to blow up. I am telling myself, "Get it out nicely." I was a pressure cooker which is about to blow up any minute.

These quotes vividly convey the sense of an enormous effort at self-overcoming in order to avoid an escalation. "The heavy locks" that lock the entire body are symbolic of both the magnitude of the energy invested and the strict limits imposed on her action. Additional effort is invested in letting out what needs to be out, in a rhythm that is not violence provoking. The pressure cooker will not explode, but the price seems to be that all the energy a woman possesses is invested in balancing and controlling the pressure. This woman has constructed her joint reality as uncontrollable and thus confines her efforts to controlling herself. The advantage of such a shift from couplehood to the self is that it restores the woman's sense of control. Though the scope of control is limited to the self, it ensures that the woman can predict what will happen as far as she can predict her own behavior. The we-ness is gradually emptied of content and signals a process of retreat from a joint life to a lonely one. When all means fail and the loss of control is imminent, women may attempt in their minds to turn the loss of control into a desideratum. This is illustrated by the following quote:

> I feel that he decides a lot. . . . He is trying to control everything, to the last detail. This gets on my nerves. I lost myself, my identity. . . . I am not a woman who likes to control. But I like it even less when I am being controlled. So I dream of a house without any control. He is not my property, and I am not his. I don't like control.

However, the withdrawal tendencies do not end with the attempt to narrow life down from we-ness to isolation but should be seen as a step toward gradual loss of control over oneself as well. Whereas previously, she was at least able to predict her own behavior, now such prediction can no longer be trusted. This is illustrated in the following quote:

> He's telling me he doesn't do it on purpose. He's explaining that this pressure comes to him . . . suddenly. That he's not in control. I can't see the things as he does. I can't even hear that. I am sick of it, I am sick of it. I am feeling that I have no more strength to handle this. This is what I feel these days, that I have no energy to handle it, and I am afraid. . . . I feel that the power I had once, I don't have it anymore. Today, I feel less control over my nerves. I tend to blow up. Yes. Today, I can pick up something and break it into pieces or turn the house upside down.

The woman in this quote clearly perceives herself at the lowest ebb, and she acts as her male partner does. In loss of control, they are similar yet not together because reconstructing togetherness clashes with their sense of being strangers to each other ("I can't see things as he does").

Estrangement is also underscored by the woman's metaphorical understanding of the essential qualitative difference between the man's loss of control and hers: Although she rejects the man's version of a sudden explosive loss of control, she suggests a piecemeal cumulative model for herself, whereby her attempts over time lead to burnout and gradual loss of this ability. By emphasizing the differences between their modes of loss of control, the conspicuousness of the difference somewhat conceals the similarity.

Last, the woman recognizes that violence became an everyday feature in her inner life as her partner succeeded in making her loss of self-control permanent. One woman said,

> Violence is usual, and it comes mostly from me . . . it fills me with guilt and anxiety and everything you can think of. . . . I feel he made me get to that point. . . . Just like him. He was looking for ways to make me loose control and become helpless, and it worked.

It can be said that the theme of control is prevalent among most if not all battered women. All battered women need to deal with control in some way or other because men introduce the control theme as central to the relationship. Once the partners accept it, the control paradigm gains a holistic and all-encompassing effect on their understanding of the conflicts and the escalation to violence. Control becomes not only an interpersonal variable but an intrapersonal variable, too. Attempts to control may lead the woman either toward managing the violence or to taking on a violent identity. Self-control, the other's self-control, and the control one has over the other's self-control all converge around the need to defend one's sense of self-respect and emotional survival.

Summary

In the foregoing chapter, we have described and analyzed the metaphors used by batterers and battered women to construct a world delineated by two taken-for-granted sets of expectations: that there will be violence and that the couplehood will continue to exist. These constructs narrow the range of personal and interpersonal operations to rigid, gender-based scripts and rituals. By these scripts, the man sometimes becomes a gender warrior, whereas the woman's way is to become a relationship manager. Although the relationship between metaphors and constructs is not linear, we can say that gender-based metaphors lead to constructs that perpetuate both violence and couplehood as endurable. However, these constructs are not static, and in the interaction between the genders, violence and couplehood gradually become increasingly rigid, to the point of severely limiting the choices partners have in their lives. Ultimately, partners become increasingly helpless and trapped.

7

Accounts of Intimate Violence

The decision to continue living together in spite of violence entails accounting for it and bridging the gap between normative expectations within the family and the occurrence of violence (Bograd, 1988). These accounts are not haphazard but rather are patterned. The content analysis of in-depth interviews with cohabiting couples living in violence leads to a structure of accounts that can be conceptualized along three continua. The first continuum is related to attempts to minimize the distance between normative expectations and intimate violence. On one end of the continuum, there are attempts to deny intimate violence, whereas at the other end, the normative expectations (the illegitimacy of violence) are called into question. When a person chooses one of these extreme options, no account is needed: There is no need to explain violence if it has never occurred or if it is legitimized by expectations. Any other point on this continuum represents an attempt to minimize either the act or the expectation. Under such conditions, although the distance between the expectations and actual acts has been minimized, there will always remain a gap, because there is no culture which overtly and completely legitimizes violence, and there is no violence that will disappear without leaving a trace. Thus, the residual gap still needs to be addressed. This is done in a way that can be represented by movement along a second continuum, one that provides legitimacy for the remaining gap. At one end of this continuum, we identify excuses, which help individuals to reject or postpone responsibility, whereas at the other end, we identify justifications, which recognize the responsibility and view the violence as an expression of this responsibility. Once the distance has been minimized and the gap bridged, the actors involved in the violence turn to damage control. An account will be successful only if the person who gives the account is able to detach the act from the actor and place the latter in a positive biographic context in which violence is but a part of his or her overall being. It should be mentioned that accounts are evaluated by those who give them according to their practical results, which may range from minimizing the negative outcomes of violence to being rewarded for the violence, which constitutes the third continuum. If the account fails and the actor is sanctioned for the violence, he or she will seek self-compensation for the failure through additional violence; if on the other hand, the account is successful, it can become an incentive to continue the violence or even increase it. It can be said that in the content of accounts, we have the seeds of subsequent violent events. In the remainder of this chapter, we describe, illustrate, and analyze each of the above continua.

Minimizing the Distance Between Normative Expectations and Intimate Violence

This continuum, ranging from denying the specific violent event to questioning the normative expectations underlying it, can be conceptualized as ranging from the narrow situational context to the broader sociocultural one.

Narrowing the Scope of Violence

The denial of violent events can be examined along several dimensions. One is a time dimension, which determines the boundaries of the event, beginning with antecedents and ending in consequences. These intervals may vary from several minutes to several months or years. Another dimension is related to the extent of the violence in terms of intention, frequency, duration, intensity, and consequences and the degree to which each one of these is overt or covert. For instance, intention may be covert and only known to the perpetrator, whereas consequences are usually more discernible. This will influence the choice of the specific point on the time axis at which an account is formed. In this sense, any account is a temporary choice that can be changed if it becomes irrelevant over time. It is therefore unlikely that the accounts given immediately after a violent event will refer to consequences, because these are more manifest hence less negotiable at that time. The third dimension is related to which agency is at the focus of the account: the perpetrator, the victim, or the couple as a unit. When the focus is on the perpetrator's intentions, the account is likely to seize onto the antecedents of the violent events; if the focus is on the victim, however, the account is more likely to concentrate on the consequences of the violent events; and if the focus is on the couple, the account will probably center on the severity of the violence.

Partners negotiate about what did or did not happen in a temporal sequence, consisting of the antecedents of the violent event, the event itself, and its consequences. Within this temporal sequence, several conditions must be met for there to be an acknowledgment of the event as violent: intentions prior to the event; its frequency, duration, and intensity; and last, its consequences.

Intentions prior to the event serve as a reliable lens through which the entire event can be usefully inspected. Accounts that hinge on intent are helpful in constructing a reality within which the violence can be interpreted as well-intended, not intended at all, or induced by normative considerations. If the redefinition along these lines is successful, the event will not be considered violent, even though it contains all the characteristics of violent events. Such events come to be classified as accidents. For example, one man claimed, "I pushed her unintentionally. She got hit by the wall, fell, and lost consciousness. You don't think I did it on purpose, it just came out this way." Another woman explained, "It may happen that he pushes, because he is in a trance . . . but he does not really mean to hit me."

The accounts of a violent act are usually made up of several components. By successfully manipulating one or more of these, through an account, the severity of the violence can be diminished and the act in question may be reconstructed as almost harmless or even as nonviolent.

Frequency: This component denotes the average number of occurrences of violent events within a given period. When the violent occurrence is presented as rare, the violence is considered marginal or even nonexistent in the couple's life. For example, "It's seldom if ever that I hit her. . . . I wouldn't call that violence."

Duration: This component denotes the length of time that the violent event lasts. As with frequency, if the duration of the violent event is short, the violence can be seen as but a lapse within a non-violent everyday life and therefore may be deemed insignificant. As one man suggested, "We are people that turn on and turn off very fast . . . so a 1-second slip . . . you can't really say that's violence."

Intensity: This is the most complex component of the violent act, for it is used in a variety of ways in building accounts. It concerns the process within a given violent event and the extent of responsibility for the damaging potential of violence. It is distinguished from frequency, which pertains to the number of violent acts over time. In addressing this component, accounts may refer to the severity of the blow itself (e.g., "hitting her gently"), the means by which the violence was done (e.g., "I would never use a weapon, just my bare hands"), or the body region chosen to be harmed (e.g., "I never hit her in the face or the head . . . just over her legs, back, or hands").

When the consequences of the violent act are considered mild, these become a gauge for evaluating the entire act. Accounts refer here mostly to visible marks on the woman's body, which can be verified. When the consequences are less visible, the violent character of a specific occurrence may be denied. For example, one man said, "I just slap her, I don't really punch her and I didn't kill her or anything."

Questioning Normative Expectations

Three such interrelated categories of accounts were identified in our data. One concerns attempts to organize norms and values into a hierarchy of importance. Here, the partners present a set of norms or values as being more important to them than refraining from violence. By so doing, they in effect define violence as relatively unimportant and therefore easily accounted for. The second category presents norms and values as having declarative rather than actual value. This means that partners state a set of norms, even though they do not live by them. Although violence may not be considered quite desirable, they are not bound by such standards. Therefore, the standards can be considered as ineffective and irrelevant. The third category comprises the adopting of an overall interpretive stance vis-à-vis norms and values. This enables the partners to reinterpret the norms prohibiting violence as if they permitted it. The following quote from a violent man illustrates these possibilities:

To tell the truth is more important than anything else. The truth holds the couple together. One doesn't necessarily have to hit his partner, but if there is no choice, than that's it. And let me ask you, who decided on these rules? Who said so? Where is it written? Who is going by it? Ask me since when you just walk into someone's house? What about people's privacy? There are people who would tell you that if you don't use force, you are violent, since by doing that, you harm the relationship. It's written [in the scriptures] "Spare the rod, spoil the child." Why wouldn't that apply to women? Is she less important than kids are? Those who wrote these things know less than we do?

Let us examine how partners use this type of account to make their joint life possible. The persuasiveness and authoritativeness of this kind of account is derived from the normative consensus that makes violence not only socially acceptable but also expected. In other words, because the violence is socially sanctioned, it is perceived by the partners as not only legitimate but as functional as well. As one man philosophizes, "A man's got to do what a man's got to do." His partner accepts violence as a normal part of her life: "There are no families without some kind of violence. If they didn't fight a little, they would be crazy. Perhaps they wouldn't tell you, but inside their house, there is pushing and shoving." Violence may now be used to enhance various aspects of the relationship, such as channeling tension, achieving contact, minimizing or increasing distance. The following quote from a battered woman encapsulates this dynamic: "We argue and all that stuff. So after a while, it explodes, there must be a fight to make all this tension break out and bring us back together." Thus, violence becomes an important means for regulating and enhancing the quality of the relationship. It should be emphasized that these accounts were seldom given explicitly, because they are recognized as being unacceptable and ineffective in a social context in which violence is condemned. They were more often discerned as a latent motif resounding in the interviews.

Legitimizing Gaps Between Violent Acts and Expectations for Nonviolence

So far, we have tried to show attempts to shorten the distance between violent acts and normative expectations. We maintained earlier that accounts used to deny the act or to manipulate the expectations minimize the distance but never overcome it completely. The remaining gap therefore needs to be accounted for. This is done by manipulating the responsibility for the violence.

According to Scott and Lyman (1968), two types of accounts have been identified in the sociological literature: excuses and justifications. *Justifications* are accounts in which one accepts responsibility for the act but denies the nefarious quality attached to it. For instance, one may admit the violent act but deny its immoral character, on the grounds that the victim deserved her fate. *Excuses* are accounts in which one acknowledges the inappropriateness of the act but denies full responsibility for its occurrence. For instance, a man may admit to having violently assaulted his wife but blames it on a loss of control over his actions. Our interviews with partners living in intimate violence showed that excuses and justifications are not separate categories but actually overlap along a continuum representing the level of responsibility. The so-called purest excuses involve total rejection of responsibility, whereas the purest justifications involve acknowledging full responsibility for the violent act. This continuum extends from excuses representing the person as passive—as one to whom things just happen—to justifications representing the person as active and as making things happen.

Any account on this continuum involves an activating mechanism comprising three conditional components that have to act jointly to provide a plausible account. First, there are some inherent personal and cultural tendencies or inclinations of the couple that are givens; second, there are circumstantial characteristics that will activate the inherent ones; third, there are situational factors that enable the occurrence of violence. Partners often use the metaphor of explosiveness to distinguish between these features. When the given characteristics are explained as the explosive, the circumstantial characteristics are the fire, and the enabling is the bringing of the explosive and the heat together toward generating an explosion.

Excusing Violence by Rejecting Responsibility

In this kind of account, violence is presented as an inevitable consequence of losing control. Loss of control has long been established as an important explanation of escalation from dyadic conflict to violence (e.g., Bograd, 1988; Coleman, 1980; Dutton, 1988; Holtzworth-Munroe, 1992; Hyden, 1994; Ptacek, 1988). Our findings indicate that there are three conditions for generating accounts based on loss of control: a short temper (a personal tendency that is a given); a stressful life (circumstantial characteristic), and situational factors (enabling violence).

Short Temper

This condition is related to individual personality traits, whereby an actor with a so-called short fuse cannot control his anger. This causes the actor to erupt immediately following a stimulus (as elaborated in the sections on the second and third conditions). The following quote illustrates this phenomenon: "It turns out that I've got the same nature as my father. . . . A short fuse. . . . He yells and yells and within 5 minutes, he calms down as if nothing had happened." Here, having a short fuse is perceived as an innate characteristic that is inherited and therefore, is beyond one's control. It is powerful, of short duration, provides relief, and dissipates directly after the reaction, when everything returns to normal.

Stressful Life

This is a more diffuse condition generated by internal interpersonal and social circumstances, such as the use of alcohol, interpersonal conflict, or unemployment. The following quote illustrates the emergence of stress as an outcome of economic hardship:

> The economic situation influences everything: stress, fights, no sex. Give me decent furniture, a well-paying job, a color TV, nothing special; just what all people have, a flat with three bedrooms, than I can live a normal life. She often admits it herself: "You and me fight only because of the situation we are in."

When a person with a short fuse experiences stressful life situations, the combined effect is potentially devastating: "When I am angry, I don't control my words or my actions. I can remember everything, but I lose control. . . . I feel pain inside, and I can tear the house apart within a few minutes." Anger and "nerves" are related to loss of control and are seen as gender-specific emotions and therefore more legitimate when exhibited by men than by women (Eisikovits & Buchbinder, 1996). Both men and women interviewed by us described themselves as becoming nervous or "having nerves." However, although men were looked on sympathetically by both spouses when losing control at the peak of a fight, women were legitimized when getting nervous but not on erupting.

Situational Factors

Situational factors are related to audiences, participants, and locations that either enhance self-control or catalyze loss of control. For instance, loss of control may take place only at home but not in front of the children. The following quote is illustrative: "The kid is one of the reasons which stops us from arguing and fighting. . . . He says to me, 'You know I won't raise my hand on you for the sake of the boy.' . . . I know I won't be hit when he's there, so I carry on. The boy is everything for him." Perceiving violence as a consequence of loss of control is functional for preserving the dyadic unit on two counts: First, it relieves the man from responsibility for his behavior, insofar as he is temporarily unaware of what he is doing. Second, loss of control occurs and ends within a short time, so it can be viewed as an episode that does not represent the man's behavior in general. As individuals who can "turn on and off very fast," they use the short duration of the violence to marginalize and normalize the violent event as a whole. Consequently, the man is considered to be generally nonviolent and thus a worthy partner (Goldblatt, 1997; Ptacek, 1988). People who use these accounts acknowledge the existence of violence in their lives but deny the responsibility for its occurrence; they see it as happening for reasons beyond their control (Andrews, 1992; Ferraro, 1983; Holtzworth-Munroe, 1992; Stamp & Sabourin, 1995). In that way, as far as the batterer's account goes, the causes for the violence are pushed outside the boundaries of the couplehood.

We found in our interviews that women used these accounts for their spouses' behavior approximately three times as much as men did for themselves. It appears that acknowledging the presence of violence is more threatening for women than for men. In the women's experience, it seems to be easier to live with a violent man who is not held responsible for his behavior, because this may answer the woman's need to explain both her partner's violence and her decision to remain in an intimate relationship with a violent man in spite of social expectations to the contrary (Loseke, 1987). The man who is legitimately violent when out of control is released from his responsibility while the woman acquires an illusion of power and control in a situation where she is otherwise powerless. It should be noted that this kind of account is frequently given to explain away problems arising in the dyadic unit that are caused by economic stress.

Once such causal links are established, they redefine violence as a symptom of distress. These accounts are therefore expected to be more acceptable to outside audiences than explanations that present violence as a function of personal responsibility. When problems in the dyad are defined in this manner, they come to be seen as universal rather than specific to violence. Violence is thus transformed into a feature of problematic families in general, rather than one of deviant behavior in a particular family. For instance, it is normative that when people face economic distress, their inner resources are challenged accordingly and are not available for coping with additional emotional difficulties. Furthermore, it is more respectable to experience problems induced by extrinsic causes than to admit the existence of violence caused by personal or interpersonal problems involving one or both partners.

Accounts based on loss of control are paradoxical and contradictory in nature: On the one hand, the couple comes to a tentative agreement that the perpetrator is unable to control his behavior; on the other hand, situational factors, such as the presence of children, are considered as mitigating factors halting the eruption of violence. Given the potential of such accounts to explain the most deadly forms of violence, it is critical to understand their tactical machinations.

Justifying Violence by Assuming Responsibility

In this category, accounts of violence are used as instruments of control by which family members are able to maintain the couplehood. Our findings indicate that three conditions have to be met for it to be possible to generate accounts based on regulating responsibility: expectations regarding differential division of roles and responsibilities (couple characteristics that are givens), violence as a legitimate means of achieving mutually desirable goals (circumstantial characteristics), and threats to the existing division of roles and responsibilities (enabling factors).

Expectations Regarding Existing Division of Roles and Responsibilities

Such expectations are the basis of togetherness, and their infringement constitutes a major challenge to the integrity of the couplehood and to the well-being of its members. The expectations of security, well-being, and joint meaning are universal in families; what is unique about those living in violence is the sense of fragility attached to these expectations.

To the spectator, the relationship may seem complementary and harmonious, but the woman is typically expected to react according to her partner's needs rather than the other way around. Everything is under control as long as the woman is fulfilling her traditional duties as expected. One man put it simply: "When I come home, I expect food on the table and to have everything ready."

The expectation of complementarity is matched by the concern that it may break at any time. The whole arrangement appears to be like a house of cards: The wrong touch on a weak spot will make the entire structure collapse.

Threats to the Existing Division of Roles and Responsibilities

Anything that interferes with the delicate balance of roles and responsibilities is interpreted as a threat and becomes a potential trigger for violence. Inherent in the fragility of the situation is the high probability that violence will occur. Paradoxically, the need for security and predictability is satisfied by the certitude that violence will indeed occur.

For example, the balance was upset between the members of a couple whose children's education was controlled entirely by the woman. The trigger for violence was her husband's attempt to change the existing arrangement by getting more involved. According to him, "She is controlling the education of the children because I agreed to have it that way . . . but she doesn't seem to remember that." In this situation, the woman is threatened by her partner's attempts to invade her territory, whereas the man is threatened by the mere idea that he can no longer decide which territory belongs to whom. Clearly, the partners are not concerned with educating the children but rather with educating one another in territorial matters.

Violence as a Means to Achieve Mutually Desirable Goals

Unique to these couples is not only their perception of violence as a legitimate means for achieving desired goals but also that they view violence as less threatening to the couplehood than the danger of losing balance of power—the underpinning of their understandings. The more interpersonal issues are felt as threatening, the higher the likelihood of violence. The possibility that interpersonal understandings will be broken is more threatening than the violence. As one man explained, "I slapped her only because the situation became risky. You know, it's my responsibility to protect us from dangerous things." His partner agreed: "He slapped me to get me back on track. . . . Who knows what would have happened without this." The dialogue between the partners achieved through violence tends toward pseudo-harmony. The man uses violence as a warning, signaling that the boundaries have been infringed and that danger is imminent; the woman acknowledges the validity of the man's position and further emphasizes that violence successfully protected her and the relationship from taking a turn for the worse. The man is responsible for making his spouse responsible. She accepts the arrangement according to which his responsibility is more pronounced.

There is a high degree of consent between the spouses regarding this hierarchical distribution of charges. The woman's extended responsibility for maintaining the boundaries is functional as a device for overcoming her helplessness and substituting it with a measure of control over the relationship. Accordingly, she feels that she can balance and manipulate the situation and that her life is not exclusively a function of her spouse's unpredictability. The division of responsibility is also functional for the man, in that it enables him to present the entire process of violent events as a joint undertaking and as such, an integral part of the couplehood. Within this framework, both partners are able to maintain a positive image and a dynamic and complementary picture of the dyad. Furthermore, from the man's perspective, keeping violence moderate and controlled contributes to ending it. By extending his spouse's responsibility to the violence, he acquires the freedom to be violent.

Much of our data on the escalation of violent events indicate that the emergence and outbreak of violent acts was well controlled and occurred within clear-cut boundaries. As a function of these boundaries, couples assigned to each other differential responsibility, authority, and role expectations, all of which contributed to framing and preserving the violence between them.

To enhance the credibility of the accounts related to regulating control within the dyad, partners need to address the issue of the threat to each other's well-being, as this defines the causes of violence and operationalizes the sense of control. The accounts can be respected on a continuum where, on one side, the woman is the target of threats; at the other end, the man is, and significant others (e.g., children) and couples as the targets are located in the middle of the continuum. We shall briefly focus on the two extremes of this continuum.

Women as Subjects of Threat

In this case, both the man and the woman recognize the existence of two previously mentioned conditions for losing control (short temper and situational factors) and attempt to cooperate in neutralizing the third one (stressful life situations) in the hope of avoiding escalation to violence. As one man warned, "It all depends on the other side; that is, I hit her, let's say I give her a slap, she'll be safer if she moves to the other room. If she does that, it all ends well." The woman is expected to manipulate situational factors so as to avoid escalation, and mild violence is used as a buffer and a warning of the severe violence to come. The woman passively concedes to the man's interpretation of the situation:

> It often happens that I say something, and I know I am right. He'll talk to me with his hands: "You don't know, you don't understand." If we keep arguing, it can get bad, very bad. Therefore, I shut up, avoid him, I'll let him calm down, pull himself together.

Men as Subjects of Threat

Here, the man feels threatened with being deprived of his natural rights, as he perceives them. To his mind, such a threat provides him with moral grounds for violence, even more so than in the previous category. For instance, one man accused his partner of interfering with his work: "She meddles in my work affairs. I don't think that's right to do. . . . She feels she has the right to manage my life. That's what I feel she's doing all day long." The man feels threatened by his partner's attempts to penetrate into his territory, pointing to a threat of loss that justifies the use of violence: "I swear that I never came home and simply hit her. I hit her only as a reaction to what she had done. . . . She had it coming, and she'll know not to do it again." Because the partner is perceived as the cause of violence, the perpetrator feels justified in using it. Furthermore, once there is a violation of the understandings that have been taken for granted, the perpetrator sees them as void and thus attempts to impose new understandings, with renegotiated roles and territories.

The spouses living in intimate violence are faced with a complex task: to maintain one's self-image as nonviolent at the expense of the other while taking into account how far they can go in blaming the other and still continuing their coexistence. To preserve their togetherness, they seek to balance blaming each other by taking some responsibility for selected aspects of the violence, its causes or consequences.

The Positive Biographical Context of an Actor: Divorcing Violence

It has been argued that accounts are given in a biographical context. This is useful on several grounds. First, positive biographical contexts may serve as an account by themselves. Second, such context lends validity to the accounts given. One's accounts are to be taken seriously if they come out of a normative biography. Third, because accounts are given to an audience, positive biographical contexts serve as "character witnesses" in favor of the person who gives them and cancel out the deviant acts. Doing justice to a violent episode takes the form of understanding it diachronically, as a marginal part of one's biography.

In this vein, we found that the couple's self-presentation as normal in spite of the occurrence of violence is the key feature of their social identity. This is accomplished by making statements that are testimonies to awareness of and adherence to social norms, without necessarily specifying the connections of these norms to violence. The combined effect of acknowledging the norm and offering an account for the violent act is like that of figure and ground, in terms of creating a positive and socially plausible and acceptable identity. It also gives credibility and validity to accounts given in relation to violence. Furthermore, by presenting themselves as part of the mainstream normative structure, both perpetrators and victims alike take a stand on their social affiliation and present this identification as an overriding background factor that regulates behavioral expectations and solidifies their credibility. The manipulation of figure and ground is functional in dealing with the violence itself. By weaving normative expectations into their depictions of the violence, the couples shift the focus from violence to the normative context in which the violent event took place, thereby rendering the violence less central. For example, one batterer stated, "No need to hit a woman. . . . Talking should solve things. It's so ugly to hit a woman."

The foregoing analysis has focused on the static and structural components of given accounts. Such an analysis emphasizes the situational aspects of dyadic life as presented in the accounts. To expand our understanding as to how the accounts work, we need to elaborate on the processual, dynamic aspect as well. The dynamics of the accounts can be conceptualized along several continua: One is related to the level of acknowledgment, ranging from complete acknowledgment to denial of the violence. Another refers to the extent of blame, ranging from self-blame to blaming the other. These two continua are part of the personal dimension. The interaction between the two results in a continuum representing the level of personal responsibility associated with the violence. Another set of continua can be derived on the social dimension. They include the level of the predictability of the world, ranging from total chaos to complete determinism, and the extent of socially sanctioned authority, ranging from strong to weak. The interaction between these two continua creates another one, that of power differential. The negotiated reality concerning violence between partners is the result of the interaction between the continua of personal responsibility and the power differential.

The interaction between acknowledgment and blame creates four mutually exclusive possibilities, constituting one dimension by which the accounts are negotiated: acknowledging the facts and blaming oneself; acknowledging the facts and blaming one's partner; not acknowledging the facts or the blame; and ambivalence regarding both acknowledgment of facts and blame. Each of the above possibilities involves a different level of responsibility for both the self and the other.

The interaction between predictability and authority leads to three mutually exclusive possibilities, which constitute an additional dimension for negotiating accounts. One is that the world is chaotic and there is no control over it. The second is that the world is determined, orderly, and fully predictable. Common to these two possibilities is that the person is not responsible for what happens in the world. The third option lies in between, and represents various combinations of chaos and determinism. These in-between possibilities provide various measures of power and control, and their extreme manifestation occurs when the individual perceives himself as "master of the universe."

As a result of the previously described interactions on the individual level, partners come to negotiate the violence (e.g., what happened, why did it happen, and what does it mean) with a certain sense of power and responsibility. Here again, there are three options: The first is what we call *mutuality,* where the partners tend to divide responsibility and there is a low level of power struggle, if any. The resulting accounts are useful for maintaining low levels of violence. The second is termed *complementarity,* involving an agreed-on subordinate-superordinate relationship in terms of power and con-

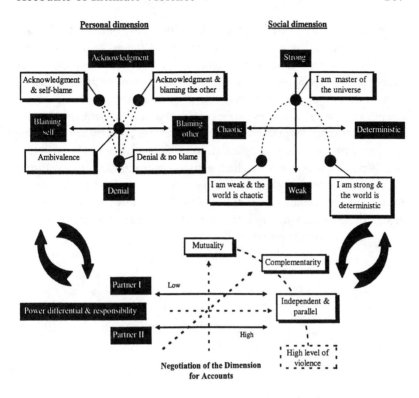

Figure 7.1. The Process of Negotiating and Choosing Accounts Over Time

trol. This is functional for accounts of the justification type (e.g., "I hit her so she won't do it again") and can be expected in cases of mild violence. The third is labeled *independent and parallel* (i.e., that there is an overt and active struggle for power and an assigning of responsibility). The accounts used under these circumstances are of the type previously termed excuses, and are likely to be found in cases of escalation to severe violence.

Summary

Given the complex structure and content of the accounts analyzed in this chapter and the dynamic interaction between the various components, a graphic summary is provided for the purpose of illustrating its various components.

Figure 7.1 summarizes the content of accounts, their structure, as well as their situational and processual variation. It appears that the

overriding theme in the accounts is the need to control the damage
produced by violence. This is possible when the accounts are structured in a manner that makes them user-friendly to the audience by
meeting their social expectations. Once past violent events are framed
and manipulated by accounts, they become guidelines for future
events and for the way these are experienced. It is noteworthy that the
way audiences interpret and react to accounts is likely to affect the
direction of violence (e.g., escalation or deescalation). This reaction
will become the context in which actors construct their reality. Either
acceptance or rejection of the accounts is likely to lead to escalation.
Only if the audience severs the violent act from the actor (e.g., we
reject the violence but not the person who was violent) is a non-
escalatory context is possible.

8

Public Exposure and Private Meaning

Battered Women's and Battering Men's Interaction With Social Agents

Life in violence tends to break out of the confines of privacy. Some features of intimate violence are exposed to social control agencies, such as the courts, the police, and social services. This chapter describes and analyzes the experiences that battered women and batterers have had with various services outside the dyad (the police and social services) and how these shaped the meaning they gave to violence. On exposure, the problem is socially reconstructed as being a result of the interaction between private and public perceptions and interpretations of the problem. Women's silence, men's justifications, and their joint accounts and rationalizations, as we described them in earlier chapters, were, prior to exposure, based on some sort of tacit interpersonal understanding, which made them familiar and predictable. When control agencies step in, these private understandings are inevitably reassessed in the light of the social definitions of the situation. These definitions include not only the interpretations of the participants but also the institutional interests, ideologies, practices, and organizational needs of the agencies that become involved. When the social control agents are contacted initially, each of the participants in intimate violence expects that his or her own version of "what really happened" will be validated and serve as the basis for subsequent action. To their chagrin, however, they discover that the results of the encounter are unpredictable. It is important to note that men and women approach the social control agencies with divergent and often conflicting hopes. In most cases, contact with outside agencies is initiated by the woman, and the man is in a reactive stance. It follows, then, that the context of the interaction between men and women involved in intimate violence and social agencies cannot be understood without examining each party's interpretation separately: Their reactions as a couple are not useful for the analysis.

Battered Women's Interactions With Social Service and Control Agencies

Battered women's seeking help should not be viewed as a single event but as a process moving in divergent directions and resultant frameworks through which the entire process is understood and given meaning. We examine these directions and frameworks and the way they are brought about.

Becoming "Helpworthy"

Most battered women interviewed by us had attempted to cope with the violence within the household over a long period of time. In previous chapters, we presented a variety of attempts to negotiate a modus vivendi with the violent partner that would rebalance the intimate relationship. At times, the actual or virtual balance becomes untenable, and partners come to believe that they have exhausted all their own means for handling their situation. Subsequently, attempts to find solutions are directed outward, and the involvement of some external assistance or control is sought. Moving beyond the intimate boundaries of the couplehood is a major turning point for both partners, as it introduces a public element into their private domain. As a turning point, such acts have a social and psychological history made up of the accumulation of difficult experiences and painful feelings and a future composed of expectations. The woman is usually the one to seek outside help, and she hopes that the official expert agencies will find the right remedy for her marriage. To understand the battered woman's experience of seeking outside help, we have to pursue the causes that she assigns to the breaking point (her moment of despair of self-help) and her expectations.

The decision to ask for outside help concludes a process of deliberation and conflict. The woman ponders over a series of opposing values and expectations. These involve circumstantially conflicting loyalties (e.g., loyalty to her family vs. loyal to herself), conflicting expectations concerning the future (e.g., will violence increase or diminish through outside intervention?), conflicting perceptions of the partner (e.g., will the seeking of help change the roles, making me the perpetrator and him the victim?), and conflicts between acting and remaining passive (e.g., leave or stay). The woman becomes inwardly active and outwardly passive. The inner dialogue takes place in utter silence but is felt as a scream. The way she sees it, breaking the outward silence by turning to social control is neither sudden nor planned but rather a further phase of the continuous inner dialogue. A woman described her decision to contact the police as follows:

> Look, you can get beaten, beaten, beaten, beaten. You don't necessarily call the police after the first event. There is a stage in which you get beaten up, again and again, and whether it is a slap or involves even guns, you don't necessarily call the police. You understand? It doesn't have to be at the peak of the beatings. You can get beaten once, twice, 13, 20 times, and there is a day on which he beats you less, and perhaps that day you'll call the police. 'Cause there comes a time when you can't take it anymore.

The severity of any specific violent act or its frequency will not necessarily lead to seeking assistance. By repeating the word "beaten" and by presenting a range of violent acts in terms of severity on one hand, and stating on the other that her reaction to these is not automatic, the woman introduces both a cumulative and a contemplative element in seeking help. The woman presents a reflective stance, describes a complex situation, and then leads the listener to the conclusion that one has to have been there to really understand. The description, in other words, is never adequate. The complexity and often contradictory nature of her experience is conveyed as if to warn the interlocutor that rational, logical means are not sufficient for comprehending what she was going through. Moreover, she expects outsiders to look beyond the experience as described and search for its hidden symbolic meaning because the very verbalization of the experience carries the danger of oversimplification.

What we have described so far can be seen as attempts by the battered woman to transform her violent experience into expectations for outside help while bridging the conflicts associated with this process. In our interviews, we found that the dominant aspiration of the battered woman who seeks help is to be empathetically validated. The meaning given by battered women to this term is that they expect outside supporters to make an attempt to relate to their narrative holistically, without rearranging it on the basis of some extraneous rationality. When this does not happen, the encounter confirms the woman's already existing ambivalence and suffering. For instance, a woman described her encounter with her social worker as follows:

> She [the social worker] had me go back over my entire history, why and what happened, and why did it happen, and how come I did nothing until now? It really threw me back to the starting point, and it broke me this week. Today, I am in far better shape, but I cried a lot during the week. I would break down in tears from any minor thing. It really hurts since you promise yourself that I would talk about this but I will not cry anymore. . . . I had lots of stop signs on the way, but I didn't stop. . . . I can only blame myself that I didn't wake up in time.

This quote illustrates that the social worker could only relate to the woman's story if it was organized developmentally and chronologically. This takes the battered woman emotionally to the past. But this woman needs help right now. She views her past as surrender and considers the soliciting of help in the present as a manifestation of strength and competence. This temporal incompatibility denies her the sense of validation and places the woman in a trap. If she accepts the social worker's ground rules, she has to deny her own experience; if she rejects them, the much-needed support will be denied.

The woman comes to the help-seeking situation in a highly vulnerable position. Any questioning of her version activates her self-doubts. She can defend herself either by withdrawing or by putting on a show of being in such an extreme state as to compel the agents to reach out to her. A woman described her interaction with the police as follows:

> The officer and the policewoman told me that he'd be arrested for 48 hours. The other policeman was waiting with my husband in the police car. The policewoman asked me, "Tell me, why did you shut up until today?" I told her I have no explanation for this. It's not like I can talk to you now with a degree of confidence and the words come out without any problem. I told her "I am retarded, I am crazy, but can I say stop?" "Yes" she said. So I told her: "I decided to say stop now, because this is the best time." I told them "don't look for

another reason. I just decided now, simply I decided to stop it. I am a limited person. Even though I am limited, can I say no? Look at it this way." The policewoman said, "I don't want you to talk about yourself like that. You are right in everything you are saying. I am sorry I asked the question. I just need to understand.

The woman in the preceding quote reflects a dual perception of herself, which is tactical. Although she views herself as a normal person, she assumes, on the basis of the police officers' questioning, that she is perceived by them as crazy. By confirming their perception of her as crazy, she provides the cue and the opportunity for the police officer to switch over to convincing her that she is sane and normal—not to worry. Overall presentation of herself obviously promotes the need to help her. It is clear from the foregoing that the battered woman's ambivalence about seeking help and her role as a person in need of support govern the encounters with the helping agents. Because she herself is not convinced, her attempts to convince the helpers are simultaneously self-persuasive and validating.

When people seek help, they assume that the mere act is a testimony to their the urgency of their needs. So the battered woman feels entitled to expect that help will be forthcoming. However, such expectations have often proved wrong in battered women's experience. Many women interviewed by us talked about the efforts necessary to secure the understanding of the police and social workers:

> I called again and again, and they still wouldn't come. In the morning, they came and arranged for him to go to the police station. I asked the police officer to come and take my full complaint and all the evidence of what I went through. He said, "I won't do it now. Someone will come in the evening and take what you have to say." What did they think? That he'll wait until tomorrow? He came home again and continued to be violent. I screamed and was hysterical. Finally, he said OK, I am coming.

Battered women know how the police operate. Only a hysterical scene will shake them out of their indifference. Their help is neither palpable nor immediate. Their rhythm is inadequate to the woman's sense of urgency. She can hope to elicit a more favorable response only by acting hysterically, but that merely reinforces the already existing stereotypes of women. She is walking a tightrope between contradictory exigencies: If she is "normal," her problem is not felt to be urgent, and if she is hysterical, her problem can be dismissed. The following quote illustrates the woman's realization that her encounter with social control is another struggle she needs to deal with:

> The problem with the police is that one police officer understands that he [the husband] is violent and another one doesn't. You need to fight them until they understand you. Can you fight them? No. But you still need to do it. 'Cause otherwise they won't do anything.

Wherever the woman turns, her life is a fight and the results are unpredictable (e.g., "one police officer understands . . . and another one doesn't"). She fought first with her partner, and then with herself about seeking help, and now with the police to make them understand her plight. This leads her to an overall sense of living in an antagonistic world in which she can take nothing for granted. Fighting becomes a way of living, without much of a support group. The woman justifies her need to fight by hoping to gain "understanding." This is a lost battle because the power balance is hopeless for the woman (e.g., "can you fight them? No"). But she still fights, because fighting has become an integral part of her (e.g., "you still need to do it"). The control agents validate her felt need to fight by making help conditional. The woman needs to persuade them by constructing her problem in categories that fit the control agents' script. Only when the woman is able to bridge the gap between her experience and the policeman's perceptions and needs does help become available (e.g., "without this, they wouldn't do anything").

Attempts to Recruit Help

A key component of the tension between battered women and the social control agencies lies in the contradictory character of the problem: On the one hand, there is the experiential definition of the reality by the women and on the other, the institutional definitions of the same, which are based on organizational needs and professional ideologies. For instance, there is evidence indicating that woman battering can arbitrarily be defined either as "wife abuse" or as "domestic disturbance" (Loseke, 1991); subsequent societal reactions vary accordingly. The following quote illustrates the ways in which a woman is forced to accept the official definition made by the police. The complaint was related to the man's throwing a cellular phone at his partner, which accidentally hit the child that she was holding:

The police told me that to lodge a complaint, it is important to go to the hospital and get a medical certificate. If I do that, they will arrest him. If I don't, they will do nothing. They told me they need to have a strong case for arresting him. They said if he would have hit only me, they would never process it. I said, "What do you mean never process it?" If it would have happened to me alone without the child, you wouldn't handle it? They said that "No, we wouldn't handle it." So I had to go to the hospital and bring them the medical certificate they asked for.

The interaction in the foregoing quote is based on a severe gap between definitions of what is sufficiently violent to warrant police intervention. The interaction is based on a power differential, which is used by the police to impose their own definition on the woman in the negotiation process. The handling of the woman's complaint is subject to police demands, which seem marginal from the woman's perspective. She is expected to adjust herself to these definitions and act accordingly, whether they seem relevant to her or not. The child becomes the focus of the complaint and is thus transformed into her source of power. The specific event becomes a lesson in which the woman learns the rules of the game for possible recurrences in the future. She is likely to draw the conclusion that the definition of danger will be based on physical injury alone and that if her complaint does not answer this criterion, there is no hope of receiving help from the police. She may also conclude that unless her suffering is medically certified, it does not exist and that her child's injury is more "usable" than her own, according to the police. The attempts to bridge this gap occur in the context of social control agents trying to educate the woman about the complaint process. To this end, the police present a series of algorithms while not necessarily helping the woman in the present or future. Variations of such user guides are provided by social service staff as well. Although the professionals perceive these guides as effective help, in the woman's experience, they are only preconditions to the actual help. When a woman implements the user guides in subsequent interactions, her expectations often remain unfulfilled, regardless of her adherence to the rules. As a battered woman said, "Nothing comes from her. Nothing! I go to her and tell her everything that is happening. She just listens and throws it back at me: 'So, what would you want to do?' She never suggested anything. Never." The battered woman is moving forward in her process of disenchantment. Implicit in the quote is the "if-then" script that was part of their initial agreement: "If you tell me everything, then I can help you." Acting on this, the woman fulfills her part by telling everything. The worker, however, throws it back at her with a new if-then script: "You tell me what you want to do, and I'll help you." Following repeated attempts to live up to new conditions for getting help, the woman is bound to realize that she will get nothing out of the relationship (e.g., "She never suggested anything. Never"). The sense of failure in the helping relationship is highlighted by divergent if not opposite expectations concerning how help should be given. For example, we found that the women expected the worker to extract from them their painful experiences surrounding the battering. The workers, on the other hand, acted on the general professional premise that if a topic is important enough, the client will bring it up. Such a discrepancy in the understanding of the helping situation was often translated by the woman as an unwillingness to help. A typical description of this process was as follows: "I asked myself, how come she does not see the beating? Maybe she does not want to talk about it. Is this the wrong place to talk about it? I'd better hide it." At this point, the battered woman may come to believe that the lack of understanding stems either from the social worker's incompetence or from her own. More often than not, the second option is confirmed by the worker. One way of reinforcing the battered woman's loss of trust in herself is by comparing her version of the narrative with that of other participants. This was justified by the professionals through the need to consider multiple perspectives. For most battered women, however, such inquiries were seen as attempts to cast doubt on their versions. Thus, their versions became one of the competing sources in a complex web of information to be used by the worker to make a so-called objective assessment of the situation.

In spite of the woman's disenchantment with the social worker, their sessions have a significant impact on the partners' dyadic life. The woman often uses the relationship with the social worker as a buffer by presenting it to the man as a source of authoritative power. As long as the partner has no contact with the social worker, this seems effective. However, the husband's threat to interfere, along with the social worker's belief that she needs to include him, threaten to neutralize this buffer. The women interviewed by us reported that by and large such encounters had negative effects on them. A woman said,

> Take my husband Shlomo. He knew I was seeing her [the social worker] at the time. He said he would go talk with her because he didn't like the kinds of shit she was teaching me. She just sat there dead scared, listened to his ugly words and said nothing. At the end she goes, "OK. I am glad I heard your version of what is going on at

home so I can better understand the situation." This was such a let-down. She asked him nothing about the beatings and the screaming at the kids.

From the husband's perspective, as understood by his partner, the social worker provided the woman with so-called forbidden knowledge (e.g., "he didn't like the kind of shit she was teaching me"), which was menacing enough for him to warrant a visit. The encounter created a new reality in which the social worker becomes a judge between two competing versions. The woman feels that her loss might be twofold: first, by losing her relative advantage vis-à-vis her partner and second, by sharing and perhaps losing the social worker to her husband. The woman who made the following statement lost her social worker both as a therapist and as a buffer between her and her husband:

> I always looked up to her. I was sure she would know how to tell him off. But instead, she was just nodding and listening to him. He talked his way out of it with her just like with me.

Once the batterer controls the social worker as he controls his wife, her ability to help the woman is neutralized. From the woman's perspective, the consequences arising from the encounter between the social workers and their partners can only make things worse:

> So they met and she asked him to tell his version of the story. He goes, "What do you mean, violent? I never ever touched her. She's lying in order to cause trouble. She wants to get back at me." After their meeting, she filled me in, and asked, "Lilly, what do you make of this? He said so-and-so and it does not square with your version. I'll have to think how can I make sense out of this mess between the two of you."

The social worker enabled the man to present his version. That way, the woman's narrative was transformed in her view from *the* version to *a* version. Because the man's version was diametrically opposed to the woman's, the social worker had to place herself above both. She reformulated the violence as an "interpersonal mess," and because the woman was her client, she placed the burden on her by asking her to help put some order into it (e.g., "Lilly, what do you make out of this?"). Given the new discoveries arising from the man's version, the worker relocates the problem in the interpersonal sphere, and thus the woman loses her as a source of support.

Disempowering the Woman Through Help

Attempts by battered women to cope with violence often center on the assignment of responsibility for it. Although in the primary stages of handling violence, battered women tend to blame themselves, they reach a point where they shift the blame to the perpetrator. This has been reported as having an empowering effect that makes for help seeking. When support agents reexamine the issue of responsibility as part of the intervention process, they are often interpreted by the battered woman as reassigning it to her. This may push her back to the starting point where she blamed herself for the violence, and it alienates her from her social worker. One woman described this as follows:

> She would ask me questions like, "Do you answer him back?" I told her I answer him as a human being who does not accept what he said or did. To hit me for this?! He can get a boxing bag. That's what I told her. She said to me, "This kind of answer would get on any husband's nerves."

Implicit in the question of the social worker ("Do you answer him back?") is the assumption that there is a relationship between her answering and potential violence. So it is up to her to forestall violence by prudently selecting her answers. The woman rejects this causal linkage and, through what is taken for sheer stubbornness, seems to validate the social worker's suspicion that her answers invite violence. By generalizing the man's reaction, applying it to all men (e.g., "any husband's nerves"), she removes personal responsibility from the man and leaves the woman solely responsible for the violence. Similar attempts to diffuse responsibility for the violence can be observed among the police. One way of doing this is by blurring the distinction between the perpetrator and victim in cases of intimate violence. A woman who attempted to seek police help stated,

> I think it is a disgrace that a police officer should tell me that "I am sick of coming here." Some police said it out loudly. The police officer called later after I complained and when I was still shaking and frightened and said, "I know what to do with you two, I will ask you both to come down. I know what to do with all these complaints." I was glad, since I didn't know what he meant. . . . Then, when we came down to the station, and he said: "OK, I know what to do with you two. I am going to make sure that the children are taken away from you.

In the woman's experience, the police regard the partners as one unit (e.g., "you two"). Repeated calls made the police "sick" of the problems this family gives them and are now willing to make this public (e.g., say it out loud). The more the violence is repeated and seeking assistance becomes a routine, the more the police develop a ritualized attitude toward the complaints as well as toward the entire violent event. This seems to work against the woman because the police tend to associate the man's violence with the woman's tendency to complain and to lump both parties together in the category of a "nagging family" that keeps giving them work. In the transformation process, the woman is increasingly stigmatized, and the characteristics of nagging and distorting become generalized into a negative attitude toward her. She is now in conflict with the authorities that are supposed to be helping her. Police intervention is now narrowed down to the threat to punish the nagging family by removing their children, which is totally unrelated to the original complaint, but may serve as a deterrent against future nagging. The message to the woman is clear: "Keep your problems to yourself, leave us out of it, because if not, your problems will be more severe." Help providers became adversaries. Such situations are not unique to women's interactions with police. They appear in similar if not identical forms in their interactions with social service workers. A woman described the difference between them and the social workers in terms of the significance that each attached to the violence: While the women experienced violence as an all-encompassing context, the social workers chose to disconnect and isolate functional problems from violence. For instance, they blurred the temporal sequence of events in the women's lives (e.g., what came first) and by so doing, the relationship between violence and malfunction in various daily activities was called into question. Problems in mothering were often a case in point.

> Lately, she started telling me, "If you can't handle the children and have no patience, we'll have to take them away from you." How could she threaten me with this? Doesn't she know they are my only reason for staying?

As the process of helping advances (e.g., "Lately, she started . . ."), the woman increasingly views her social worker as a threat. Her last line of defense is her children. When her ability to care for them is called into question, the focus of the conflict is changed, and she now finds herself struggling to keeping the children rather than handling her partner's violence. The danger of losing her children is her weak spot, and the police also use it against her:

> "I will make sure to take the children away from you. . . ." How can they tell me such things after I've suffered for so many years, and my husband just sits there and enjoys every minute of it. How can you, as a police officer, tell me that you will hurt me in order to make me stop complaining. . . . Why don't you take this bad thing [her partner] instead of my children. That's why they pay you." So he'd tell me, I never told you that I'd take the children. You are distorting things. Probably that's the way you distort things about your husband when you complain.

In the battered woman's experience, she is administered blow after blow: She is first beaten, then threatened with losing the children, and last, she is regarded as unreliable because of distorting and exaggerating everything. Under such conditions, she is made to believe that whatever happened and is about to happen is justified. Moreover, she is now left to the mercy of her husband while the very people who were supposed to help her become handy instruments in his attempts to terrorize her:

> Zadok, my partner, is constantly threatening the children that he'll go to the social worker and tell her that I keep them hungry, I neglect them, and thus they will deny the children from me and take them away from me. The kids are shaking from fear. I told my adolescent daughter that the only thing that could separate us is if I die. You have no reason to be concerned, just tell the truth. She is afraid that if she'll tell them that she's suffering from her dad, they will take her away.

From this quote, we learn that the men know how to use the welfare services to their own advantage. They know what the criteria are for various actions that the services can take and what evidence they need to frame their partners. The woman also appears to be familiar with the ways of the system but she is terrorized by the threat, and in the process of reassuring her daughter, she intensifies her fear and terror. By using extreme situations (e.g., only death could separate us) the woman attempts to comfort the child while at the same time frighteningly alerting her to the severity of the situation. The process of seeking outside help became a fiasco for the battered woman. Instead of freeing her from her partner's violence, it further entrapped her.

Empowering the Woman Through Help

So far in this chapter, we have addressed the battered woman's sense of failure in seeking help. We have attempted to show how various help services are perceived by the battered woman as being against her. Alongside such experiences, our interview material included success stories as well. One woman said,

> The truth is that the social worker told me about these protection orders more than a year ago. But I wasn't strong enough to go through with it. I was afraid. I was constantly afraid that if I'll get a protection order, he'll murder me. One day, I said that's it. I start doing it. When I decide, I'll go all the way, that's what I did. Suddenly, I had enough strength.

Another woman stated the following concerning police intervention:

> He's got all these complaints against him at the police. But I think they wouldn't take me seriously, 'cause I didn't take it seriously in the past. That is, I told them in the past, just give him a warning. But this time, I said, you must put an end to this.

Both women highlight the importance of timing in their ability to get help. To transform the available assistance into a resource that helps them to cope with violence, women need a level of strength and decisiveness that is not always there throughout the process. The woman first quoted distinguished between a previous time when she wasn't able to use the information provided by the social worker and the present when she felt strong enough to act decisively in spite of the potential dangers. The second woman quoted makes the same argument concerning police intervention. From a position of strength, the woman is capable of contemplating the possibility of defining the actions of the helping agents as detrimental if she is too weak to take advantage of them. Such a position indicates a movement from surrendering to help, to actively seeking and using it. Strength is crucial for successful help seeking. But we must remember that the woman's acquiring strength ought to be a top priority of the helpers who want her to be able to use them.

When women experienced the welfare and social services as a source of power and encouragement, they were able to present them to themselves and to others in a positive light. One woman said,

When I have trouble with him, I go straight to the welfare office. When she [the social worker] sits with me and I talk to her, she tries to consult with me about what to do. When he would raise his hands to me, she would tell me, "Don't give up," and this gave me lots of strength and security.

Another woman said about her experience with police,

He told me, "You are now in the hands of the police, and from now on, no one will dare touch you, hit you. You are no one's object. You're no one's dog." I remember his words. "From now on, you raise your head and feel you are a human being. And no one will be allowed to do things like he did to you." It was really nice to hear that. It gave me strength . . . and I feel this sense of security up to this day. Sometimes, when it is bad, I hear his words in my ears, that no one has the right to touch me even if he's my husband.

We have attempted to show so far that the battered woman's decision to seek help is a consuming process that requires much energy and power. The woman comes to the situation in a highly vulnerable position with the initial expectation of receiving validation for her grievance. At this juncture, she may become disenchanted and disempowered and fall back into the vicious circle of violence with her partner, or she may break out of the pattern and seek additional help in becoming empowered. The direction chosen will be a function of her own strength and the willingness of the helping agents to validate her. The combined effect of these two factors is likely to guide her in the chosen direction. Once this is done, the entire helping situation will be perceived accordingly as positive or negative and will in turn strengthen the chosen direction.

Batterers' Interactions With Social Service and Control Agencies

Batterers, unlike battered women, seldom initiate any contact with the social services and control agents. They react to rather than collaborate with any attempts to hold them responsible or to help them. However, men's perception of the aims and authority of control and treatment agents is differential, as is their reaction toward their work. The batterers' perception of the police differs so greatly from that of the social service personnel that separate analyses are warranted.

They react to social workers and therapeutic intervention in general as a matter of choice. Thus, when involved in such intervention, they focus on how to use it to advance their agendas. Police intervention is imposed by their partners and leaves little choice. So now, they are focused on survival.

Batterers' Understanding of Therapeutic Intervention

Most themes emerging from interviewing batterers reveal that their perceptions of therapeutic intervention can be conceptualized along two dimensions: One concerns the unit of intervention (the man himself, his partner, or the couple); the other pertains to the impact of the intervention on him (helpful, meaningless, or harmful).

The most common attitude of batterers to any form of therapy is to resist or reject it outright. One man said,

They suggested that I go for marital counseling. But I don't really believe in it. I say, we either get along and we are able to solve our existing problems, or if we can't solve them together, it is doubtful that someone else would. . . . It's natural that two people who grew up in different houses and have such different habits and characters, when they move in together in the same household, there must be an explosion. But if we want to be together, we must adjust to each other and compromise a little with each other. . . . I simply don't believe in getting help. 'Cause I know my wife better than any counselor, and she knows me to the same extent. All in all, it depends on the person.

Another man said, "I felt no need to ask for help. 'Cause I think that no one can persuade me. If I know something one way, that's the way it is. No one can change my opinion." The men quoted here emphasize several values that are important in understanding their attitudes toward intervention. First, there is affirmation of self-sufficiency of the couple. Such a principle is functional in at least two ways: It makes the woman an accomplice to the violence but also in the search for a solution; it suggests that the couplehood is an autonomous unit that has all the knowledge and skills to solve its own problems, making external intervention superfluous. In the second quote, the concept of autonomy and self-sufficiency refers to one person: the man. By narrowing the focus, the man succeeds in keeping the power to himself. Thus, any help is pointless and if ventured, will be taken for an attack on his power position. Second, the man places willpower at the center of the remedial attempts. Self-sufficiency and willpower create an illusion of existential freedom and power to be in control of one's destiny. Simultaneously, men emphasize personal traits as central to solving the problem and thereby stress the deterministic nature of the situation. At this point, the situation is defined as easy to solve using their own resources and yet as not soluble at all because it is predetermined. Both cases make intervention futile. By minimizing the violence and placing it under control, the focus is diverted away from it to willpower; by making it a matter of destiny, willpower is rendered irrelevant. Third, where there are individual as well as family differences, there is a tendency to normalize violence as structurally expected. Once explosive behavior comes to be perceived as natural, any attempt to interfere with it is against the rules of nature. Intervention is perceived by most men as a procedure for setting right something that is broken, sick, or unnatural. If violence is explained as a natural consequence of differences arising from one's background and dependent on one's free will, there is nothing broken. And if it ain't broke, why fix it?

Given the described frame of mind of the batterers, the prevalent belief among them is that attempts to impose treatment of any kind are doomed to failure. As one man said,

> I am telling you that coercive treatment is worth nothing and will never work. Because whatever is done against your will and you have no motivation to it, you'll never want it. And even if you'll force it on me, you'll never get 100% efficiency . . . perhaps 40%, 30%, and so what did you achieve then?

This man again uses arguments related to will and motivation while introducing quantitative measures in his efficiency model. He tries to calculate in percentages the chances that the investment in coercive cures will fail, thus proving that it does not pay off. He also presents success or failure in rigid and dichotomous terms: either total (100%) success or if any less, then a failure. By predicting failure of treatment, he negates its feasibility. When the possibility of coerced intervention is considered, it is presented as mandatory for both partners. A man said, "I want them to force us to do treatment. They should send both partners to coerced treatment. So that neither partner can get away from coercion." Once the problem is shared and located in the partners rather than in him, intervention is expected to focus on the couple and the relationship. A man said,

> I feel there is some improvement, . . . that the treatment helped. All things that need to be improved, we'll work on them, we'll work on

them strongly. Even if a couple are 60 years old, there is always room for improvement. Treatment helped me to understand what was her problem. I need to help her to calm down. . . . Today, I am more calculated, understand her more, hear her more. . . . I learned to listen first, then react, and always look for her better side. And stay away from exploding and getting violent.

Several important criteria by which men assess the success of intervention emerge from this quote: The man uses a joint identity in attempting to deal with the violence. This distributes his essential responsibility and makes his partner an indispensable objective of the intervention process. He defines the treatment as an opportunity to improve a situation that was not necessarily bad to begin with. He further normalizes the situation by placing his "improvement" in the context of lifelong learning and development (even when he's 60). Last, he considers the changes achieved in treatment (being calm and considerate and calculated) as aimed at calming the woman rather than at handling his own violence. The man places indirect blame on his partner and makes her the focus of intervention. He needs to keep her calm to stop her from making him violent. Once the causes of violence are located in the other partner or the couple, the implication is that whatever will happen in the future is her fault or, at most, their joint responsibility. The intact family becomes an important element in men's strategy to fend off personal responsibility and thus is viewed as a measure of success in any form of therapeutic intervention. In relation to this, one man said,

The social worker knew that she [his partner] wants to divorce me and sue me, and that she is fed up with life with me, our financial situation, everything. So she came and listened to me and tried to find a compromise, which will bring peace between us. That was sort of good and helped us to cool out.

Another man said,

We went together to try to rehabilitate our marriage. In the beginning, there were ups and downs, but when they treated her, they found out that she was really insecure, and thus they came down on her real hard, and the devil came out of the bottle, and today she is like hell. She views me as some sort of creature which needs to be kicked, destroyed. . . . After going to be treated, she stated that she is sick of being the family dummy and that she likes herself. I am completely helpless in this. I want to rehabilitate and have no ability to do it.

These quotes illustrate that in the man's view, intervention geared to finding a compromise and keeping the framework of the family intact is rated as effective, whereas intervention that empowers the woman to identify her strengths is viewed as dangerous and leading to potentially devastating results. This reinforces the man's attempts to minimize the problem, to find ways of bridging the conflict, and ultimately, to impose his own view on the treatment situation. Good treatment should not hurt, should refrain from assigning personal responsibility, and should preserve the man's original position held when entering the treatment situation.

We have shown that the man attempts to manipulate both the unit and the impact of intervention to achieve his goals. This may range from completely neutralizing its potential effects (by shifting focus to the couplehood or the partner and defining the intervention as useless or harmful) to making these into tools for achieving his goals (by focusing intervention on the woman, trying to emphasize her problems and to enhance his power).

Batterers' Understanding of Police Intervention

In the content analysis of our interviews with batterers, we found that they reconstruct their relationship with police throughout their encounters, from the attempts to validate their normative identity, through struggling with being transformed into criminals, and finally adopting the victim identity. The changes taking place can be conceptualized according to many dimensions, including the man's perceptions of himself, the partner, the dyadic unit, and the police.

First Encounters With Police

When battered women turned to the police for help, the men almost invariably responded with surprise. They were unable to identify any difference between the act for which police were called in and other day-to-day conflicts that did not trigger such a reaction. A man whose partner called the police for the first time described an argument related to the use of the family car:

> I said, I need the car, and if I don't go out, she shouldn't either. This was the trigger. Ruth called the police and said that I threatened her and that I wouldn't let her leave the house. . . . There was no trace of physical violence nor any specific verbal violence, except the argument about the car which we have all the time. Oh, I almost forgot. I was accused of threatening, that I threatened her with a gun. And

then I said, "My God, that's impossible. I haven't had a gun for 6 months now." At some point, Ruth hid the gun from me. And this was the only thing I could say.

The man quoted here used selective inattention as to the details concerning the event, decontextualizing it to cover up the violence. For instance, the fact that his partner needed to hide the gun and the reasons for such an act are mentioned only in passing, and thus the overall context in which a seemingly trivial act is used as a "trigger" remains in the dark. The man interprets his wife's complaint as an irrational overreaction arising from a purposeful distortion of his intentions. He seems either unable or unwilling to be sensitive to the emotional climate in which his partner acted. Because the man has been taken by surprise, he can affect a certain level of disorientation and present the situation as discontinuous. He expects that the police investigation will clear it up, vindicate him, and help return life to its normal course. Being surprised plays an important role in men's perception of both the meaning of violence and the subsequent meaning of the police intervention.

When first faced with police intervention, a pseudorational model of thinking guides the men. A man described his view of the first complaint:

Man: It all started with an argument we had. At some point, I grabbed her throat, not to choke her or anything, just to shake her up. She went to the room and locked herself in. I heard she was calling the police and said, "My husband is threatening me." . . . I can't remember if she said that I threatened to murder her or not, but she said she wanted them to come right away and then silence.

Interviewer: What did you think at the time?

Man: Nothing, I said they should come to me, and I was clear that they knew that there are two sides to the story. I was waiting for them downstairs, I was watering the lawn. . . . I couldn't see anything lethal in what I did since I wasn't going to harm her. . . . I understood they would come, ask some questions: "Who are you? What happened? How did it happen?" And that's all.

Another man said,

I can't remember too many details, I think someone made a stupid mistake by calling the police, and the police is making the stupid

mistake of keeping up the game. . . . All in all, I expected that this
whole thing would come to an end by nothing. What you would call
false allegations.

Both men expected the police to assume that their acts were within
rational boundaries and therefore not dangerous. The first man successfully distanced himself from the occurrences (e.g., he watered the
garden while waiting for the police) and saw this as a testimony to his
innocence. The expectation was that the police would investigate to
validate their versions, ascertaining that there was no intention to be
violent, and that the power struggle was momentary, accidental, and
mutual. If this scenario were actualized and the police did not pursue
the matter further, there is a likelihood that life would return to normal, without the incident leaving any trace on the dyadic life. The second man defined police intervention as irrational and termed it a
stupid mistake committed by all who were involved. Using the legal
term, *false allegations,* adds a sense of injustice associated with the
so-called mistake.

For men who have such attitudes concerning the process, subsequent police investigations tend to appear as technical, routine, cere-
monial, and generally meaningless. Batterers go through the motions
without experiencing the process; rather, they focus on its conclusion
(e.g., "It needs to be done, let's do it and get it over with"). Another
man described his first police contact as follows:

> There was a police investigator who wanted to hear my version and
> my wife's. I explained my side, I explained what I know what took
> place at the time of this argument, . . . he never told me anything bad
> regarding what I said, and actually, we had it wrapped up in really
> general terms. I can't remember him saying something specific. Just
> sign here, sign there. I didn't see in the signing anything specific.
> What they made me sign is that I wouldn't threaten her. Because I
> never threaten anyway, I had no problems with signing. I can't
> remember all the details. It looked pretty meaningless to me.

What is important in this quote is not so much the content but
rather the underlying tone and mood. The man describing his first
encounter with the police displayed a rather technical interest in both
sides. His bearing conveyed that he and the investigator were merely
doing their jobs and formalizing the situation by signing. Also, there
was nothing specific to remember, so the event is recorded in his memory in general and bland terms. The man was left with a script that was
already known before the event, with no surprises, narrated in the

form of a predictable sequence of boring occurrences. The smooth and eventless atmosphere of the police investigation reinforced the man's belief that there was no violence and that he was cleared of these allegations, thus keeping his self-image intact.

Police personnel were evaluated in the light of their attitudes toward the incident. For instance, a police officer defined by a batterer as "really OK" said,

> Listen, I don't think it pays off to get into these things. . . . Think twice. It's better to get up and leave rather than get entangled. . . . You saw you are getting pissed, get up and leave. Turn around and go. Return in 2 hours. Every small touch, or even if you don't touch her, just verbal violence, can get you in trouble. And to write you up and fill in all these forms and have a record doesn't fit you. So go home, get some clothes, and leave for a couple of days.

The "good policeman" is the one who teaches the man how to stay out of trouble without confronting him with the allegations of violence. The discussion is diverted from the investigation of the violent act to the avoidance of its recurrence. In the man's view, the police officer further legitimizes his good standing and self-image by warning him of the potential consequences of being accused. In addition, the man understands the rules of the game regarding being a suspect, where even a "single touch" or word can be interpreted as violence. He uses the dramatic language appropriate to his status as a suspect to present the actual violence and the actual institutional response to it as grossly exaggerated. This enables him to redefine the situation so that he now is in danger of becoming the victim of an injustice and that his wife's complaint is the source of it. The first encounter with the police reinforces in the man the belief that his violence cannot be confirmed, that his situation is due to exaggeration and distortion, and that the police investigation tends to confirm his version of the reality.

In general, the confirmation of his normative identity has been an important component of the man's interaction with the police. One man stated, describing his first encounter with the police,

> The first time they came here, they wanted to arrest me. The policeman persuaded her [his wife] to cancel the complaint. 'Cause if I would have had a police record, I would have lost my job. He [the policeman] understood and identified with me especially when he saw that I am not some sort of criminal and have no criminal record, that I look like a nice guy and that I work . . . so he suggested, "Why don't you two make up and let's finish this thing."

By constructing his normative identity, the man forged a temporary alliance with the police. Once such an alliance is established, the man becomes "one of us" rather than "one of them," and thus he dissociates himself successfully from the potential clientele of the police. The violent event is marginalized, and his overall normative identity becomes the background against which his behavior is examined. A case in point is the weighing of his actions within the context of his career. This is a major gender imperative by which all men are socially evaluated. The man is reinforced in his perception of his partner in an adversary position. A man described an isolated occurrence, for which police were called in by his partner:

> When she started screaming and swearing, I got pissed and threw the garbage can at her. I didn't mean to throw it, but in that situation I did it, and it hit her. She made this big thing about it and called the police and said I raised my hand to her. A policeman and a policewoman came, and I told them my version, she told them hers. . . . The policeman took me aside and asked, "For this kind of stuff, you call the police?" Ever since, when she gets pissed, screams and swears, I know she is waiting for me to raise my hand. . . . All she needs is an excuse. She herself told me some time ago, "If I go to the police, you'll never get into the house again."

This quote reflects men's inner logic according to which, by denying their partner's basic claim that they are violent, the turning to the police would look superfluous. This is effected by focusing on her provocation rather than on his reactions and by blurring the boundaries between violent intent and violent action. From among all events taking place in the situation, the man chose to focus on the police's minimizing the event, thus providing further support to his version (e.g., why call police for such an unimportant event?). Thus, the woman's calling the police becomes a provocation and is a testimony to her hostility.

Once the police become involved in the conflict, their presence will remain in the couple's collective consciousness long after they have left. The man who has successfully dismissed the possibility that the police were called in direct response to his violence will perceive all future conflicts as aimed at provoking him sufficiently to warrant police involvement.

Second Encounter With Police

For most batterers, the second interaction with the police induces a qualitative change in their overall perception and attitude toward the police. A man described the difference as follows:

In this case, no one really talked to me at all. They told me simply, "You come with us to the station." I was really angry. The first time they were really nice to me, they told me to come to the station in my own car. The second time around, they did it all public, ugly, and ordered me around: "No, you won't drive your car, you'll come with us." You get in the car like someone who is arrested, it's really shameful.

Both the limitations of his freedom and the public nature of the arrest were counter to all the expectations that the man had formed during his first contact with the police. This placed him in a position of powerlessness and humiliation. The second interaction with the police put the batterer in the role of a suspect. He now perceives a change in the situation but still focuses on the inappropriateness of the police officers' behavior and his anger about it, rather than on his violence, which was the reason for police intervention. He still rejects the idea that he is an offender and uses the metaphor of "as if" when describing himself in custody. But he gradually realizes that he is in trouble. As one man said,

The first time, they listened to me and understood me. I wasn't offended and I was satisfied. The second time, they were unwilling to listen, they only heard my wife. I was feeling they are not interested in helping me. I didn't like it and felt helpless. I felt there is a powerful system which works against me. . . . I felt they did injustice to me, since I never beat her. I felt the police are looking for ways to get people. The minute she went to police, they believed her. The case is sealed: She speaks the truth and I am a liar.

As the man sees it, the woman's second complaint blocked the effective dialogue with the police that he had had during the previous encounter. Whatever he says becomes irrelevant, because the police have already found him guilty and the interaction is geared toward substantiating this finding. He feels quite alone, vis-à-vis forces that are both large and hostile. Such a reading of the situation places him on the defensive. He also comes to redefine the "system" as an insurmountable and machinelike bureaucracy. Within this context, the woman partner appears as the one who has the power to activate the bureaucratic machinery against him. Now, he is at the woman's mercy. The following quote exemplifies this belief:

This policeman took me down to the station and told me, "That's how women are, don't get into trouble. They are out to get you. Just like men are looking to catch women and cheat on them, the woman is out to get you on this one. She'll prepare your case for court."

Police activity at this point conveys a double message to both partners. To the man, as shown, they simultaneously convey the message that he is in trouble and that this second time around, the rules have changed. But they are still giving him friendly advice as to what he can expect from women. To the woman, as seen in the following quote, they convey that the decisions are up to her, though she should be aware of the price of going ahead with the complaint.

> **Man**: When my wife sat with the investigating officer, he was telling her that since this is the second time, he'll arrest me and put me in jail. Actually, this scared her. . . . He suggested to her to let the whole thing go, and let it be.
>
> **Interviewer**: Did someone come and tell you that you'll be arrested since it is the second time?
>
> **Man**: Not really. I'll tell you, they tried to persuade Sarah to let this story drop, since it is not worth it, since I may get hurt, and my job may be affected. I also think he explained to her that she doesn't have a good case and all she can get out of this is to scare me.

By what they say and how they say it, the police personnel simultaneously provide the message that even though they think the man was violent, they also think that the woman would hurt the man by complaining. In the former quote, the man was told that he would be handled roughly if complained against again, and simultaneously, he was cautioned to beware of his partner as an enemy. In the latter quote, he is reminded by the police that he can go to jail, but at the same time, they act as his advocates in pleading with the woman to cancel her complaint. Instead of deterring the man, the police deter the woman. If there is no case for arrest, why is there a threat to arrest him? If there is a case, why do they threaten the woman that his arrest might result in undesirable consequences for her? Between these conflicting messages, the man ends his second encounter with the police confused, on the defensive, and with a sense that things are serious this time. Even so, there is the feeling that his chances are still good if his partner can be appeased. This hope is further strengthened when the man perceives the police as being caught in the dilemma of having to react to the actuality of the violence while also having to consider the price the family will be forced to pay. One man said,

> I know how they think. They think she wants to hurt me with these complaints, but on the other hand, they know that ultimately we'll

make up and she'll come home, and the result will be that she's hurt me with these legal procedures.

In other words, to the last, the batterer exploits the police's hesitant reaction to domestic violence.

Following the second encounter with police, violent men are faced with a new question, which is related to their own identity: Are they criminals or not? They face this haunting question at a disadvantage. In the previous encounter with police, their normative identity was used as a basis for demonstrating that they are not inherently violent; rather, their partners are provocative. This time, however, the police make it plain that their normative identity is precisely what is at issue, for they are suspected to be criminals. A man described his encounter with the police thus: "Two police cars came. As if I murdered someone. . . . When they saw that I am clean and I have no criminal record and no files, one car with two policemen returned to the station. . . ." Or another man said,

> When we walked into the station, the officer asked the other policemen whether I was violent against them? I was shocked! Where did he get the idea that I am a violent man? And he said immediately, "Book him."

At this point, the man becomes conscious of the gap he will have to bridge between the social identity of a criminal being attributed to him and his self-perceived normative identity:

> The man's got a problem, too. He's got feelings, he is human, he's got respect, he's in a crisis. The police are just making it worst. . . . Instead of helping him to change his violent style, they make it worst. To relate to a man like he's a drug addict or a criminal humiliates him worst. . . . It would be better not to arrest the man, not to reprimand him and humiliate him, but send him right away to treatment.

The man opts for the role of the patient, preferring the need for help to social retribution. To some extent, to need treatment is not as reprehensible as to be branded a criminal. Or this is how the minds of very sensitive batterers work. He views the police as responsible for the role in which he has been cast and the imposition of the role as further evidence for the circumstantial nature of his deviance.

In men's experience, the negative effect of police intervention is likely to spill over into the dyadic relationship. The following quotes illustrate the effect of the woman's testimony on the marital relationship, as perceived by the man:

> She said I am endangering the children's lives and other horrible
> stuff about me as father and husband. I felt really humiliated. As a
> consequence, I was handed a protection order and was ordered to
> stay away from my place of residence. This initiates a thousand
> thoughts of vengeance.

Another man said,

> I was really upset. We've been living together for 14 years. Perhaps, I
> made a mistake once. For this, they file criminal charges against me?
> That a woman should complain against her husband for no reason.
> . . . To give untrue testimony, not what actually happened. Her testi-
> mony to the police has destroyed me.

In the first quote, the man realizes that his partner demonized him and
that her complaint is not the result of a specific event but rather of her
cumulative experience with him. He realizes that the specific explanations and causes related to one event will not be effective, because they
are viewed as only partial testimony to his total viciousness. This
appears to him as both threatening and traumatic because it attacks his
core self-image. The man is therefore left with the option of widening
the gap between himself and his partner to protect his self-image. In
the second quote, the complaint is perceived as destroying the continuity of the dyadic relationship. A 14-year relationship is at stake. To
emphasize the danger, the man contrasts the isolated violent act with
14 years of peaceful togetherness. This emphasizes the unreasonable-
ness of the woman's decision to complain and casts doubt on the
endurance of the relationship. The legalistic and formal nature of the
intervention, along with the perceived discontinuity and irrationality
of the act of complaining, brings the man to the conclusion that he was
betrayed.

Turning to the police has changed the balance of power between
the partners, and the man feels that he is in a position of inferiority:

> I really got hurt from this. Perhaps because I can't forgive her for
> this. At times, we have misunderstandings. I would throw in words
> such as "shut up." . . . But today, I have no trust in her, and perhaps
> she'll put me in jail again and do me injustice. I feel deprived.

The man perceives himself as being in danger and thus needs to be
constantly on guard. The complaint serves as a control over what he
can say and do. He feels he has lost his freedom along with his trust in
his partner. He attributes to her the power to control his freedom and
generalizes from the specific situation to his entire life. He is focusing

on his fear, which feeds his growing anger. Even when police intervention forces him to reflect on his violent behavior, there is still much ambivalence concerning the entire intervention:

> Interviewer: How did the police intervention affect the relationship with your wife?
>
> Man: It had a bad effect, both the process and the way they handled me and related to me. On the other hand, I asked myself, why did I let myself degenerate to this point? And I was thinking that even though she made a mistake, even if she was wrong, I have to control the situation and not get to the point of the police being involved. . . . I don't accept it, but I put up with it. I closed this thing and I don't want to look back. A clean start. I am not angry with her, but it is an open wound. I also blame myself 'cause I brought it on myself.

The contradictions are evident in the foregoing quote. Although he takes responsibility and reflects on his behavior, he still believes that his partner's mistake determined the way police handled him. He attempted to develop some measure of wisdom from the events, but the pain, the "open wound," overshadows the relationship. The best he can do is force himself to live with it but he can never accept it.

Repeated Encounters With Police

The gap between the batterer and his surrounding world is widening. He is increasingly alone vis-à-vis the cooperation between his partner and the police. He is more and more restricted by extraneous rules that determine his life. The police are less and less understanding. He is gradually moving toward the victim identity.

One man said,

> The problem I've got is that my wife has backing from the police. And the backing is often used to break my will . . . to show me that she is stronger than me. That's the issue. Not that she actually needs them for anything."

The man comes to believe that police intervention is sought by women to acquire power and control over him. Once the situation is reduced to a power struggle, the reality of his partner's pain is lost and substituted by the need for regaining control and getting even. Calling the police is perceived as a violent act directed against him. He feels isolated and presents his partner as being in coalition with antagonistic forces, which are stronger than he is. Although such isolation leads to a sense of injustice and legitimizes the need to fight it, it also helps the man to save face: It is not his partner alone that has betrayed and humiliated him but a coalition of which she is but a part. The coalition is socially sanctioned by rules over which he has no influence.

The police are perceived by the man as locked into a series of organizational and legal constraints that ultimately all turn against him. Although he understands the need to keep these rules and understands the way they operate, he still feels anger and injustice concerning their influence on his personal life. A man explained this as follows:

> The law defends the woman. In this country, everything is carried to an extreme. The law has to defend the woman since she is weak, and this leads to a situation of discrimination against us [the men]. I guess, reverse discrimination makes us men as discriminated against, and you have now a situation in which you have two things to fix instead of one. . . . It's a dictatorship. Where is the democracy here? They [the police] say, "We have no authority to change it, we have no responsibility, we cannot jeopardize ourselves. If something will happen to her, we would have to pay with our heads."

In the man's mind, police intervention takes place according to a preconceived scenario that has nothing to do with the facts, with the truth, or with a willingness to investigate in good faith or take all the evidence into account. Also, it appears that the man experiences the situation in extreme terms, which are not negotiable. This is expressed in totalitarian and antidemocratic metaphors, which place him in an oppressed class, that of his gender. The police are viewed as inflexible and impotent in using their own rules, if one considers how they justify their actions: "We have orders and rules, and thus we can't help it." They have no way to understand the man. Their rules and rigidity force them to sacrifice the family. One man said,

> I am simply helpless. Even if I decide to rehabilitate the relationship, and I am trying hard, no one is willing to give me a chance. Rather, they tell you to do it the other way around. They would say just go, leave the family, leave everything. That's the best solution for them. . . . But I said to myself, "I will not give in, I have children, . . ." and they kept saying, "You are stupid. Leave it all, why would you need

all this?" The whole system is geared today to destroy the marriage.
. . . It's weird.

The man attempts to redefine the meaning of his dyadic relationship following police intervention. The involvement of the police is transformed in his mind into the cause rather than being a consequence of the deterioration in the relationship. His efforts are concentrated on preserving what is left after such a breach of trust. Introducing an emotional component in his account, the man dwells on the potential harm brought on the children if he gives up the struggle to save the integrity of the family. By being a savior and "sacrificing" himself for the children, he presents himself as fighting against all odds. His partner is perceived as being vengeful toward him and indifferent toward the children.

As a consequence of the man's repeated experience with the police, he gradually constructs a victim identity. One man said,

> We men live in fear. It's impossible to live like that. When a woman gets into this "trance" of craziness, she can make the man into a rag. She is using this dry legal stuff, and she puts pressure on me, keeps me in an unbelievable fear. I live in fear, I am insecure, I am weak. I never used to be like that. I feel defeated, I am nervous at work, and it makes me crazy.

The man's sense of entrapment increases with every police visit: He is alone, misunderstood, betrayed, unable to communicate with his partner, and caught up institutionally in legalistic and dehumanized definitions of the situation. When the next encounter with police comes, his victimization rather than his violence will be the focus of the interaction.

The batterer perceived his first encounter with the police as validating his normative identity. This enhanced his sense of power and control over his partner. Although the police were called into the family by the woman, they left as the man's advocate. In spite of unwanted outside interference, the man, empowered by his initial experience, constructs a reality of a strengthened family. During the second encounter, much to his surprise, the man's normative identity is called into question by the police. The power balance is established, as the woman acquires power at his expense. Additional encounters with police reinforce this tendency, pushing the man toward a victim identity.

Summary

Exposure of the family environment to outside agents has a powerful effect on the dyadic unit and its members and shatters their personal, interpersonal, and social reality. The exposure transforms the dyadic dialogue into a social multilogue. The family members view the outside agents as new and unconventional means by which they can foster their individual goals against each other. Although the initial expectation is that these helping agents will break the circle of violence, they are constructed by the dyad as a means in their new struggle, in which each party attempts to acquire more so-called weapons in his or her arsenal. This brings the conflict to a new and qualitatively different level of escalation, which in retrospect adds justification to the presence of the outside agents.

9

Guidelines for
Intervention

This chapter presents a series of guidelines based on an existential-phenomenological orientation intended for professionals intervening in cases of intimate violence. Because intimate violence is a relatively new field of practice and research in the human services, it entails far more unknowns than certitudes. Therefore, there is a need to develop models of practice that will enable a constant contribution while securing an ongoing interaction between application and research. Given the state of the art in this domain, we believe that practice should be guided by a reflective stance (Schon, 1983), which makes the ongoing interactive learning process possible. This involves the planning, use, and evaluation of knowledge, with an emphasis on values and ethical concerns. Accordingly, practitioners constantly produce, apply, and revise their knowledge in the light of their practice. These are conceived as encapsulating the intrapersonal, interpersonal, social, cultural, and political forces involved in understanding, constructing, and attempting to control the social problem of woman battering.

In defining such a therapy, Spinelli (1997) wrote,

> Therapy, at its most fundamental level, involves the act of revealing and reassessing the "life stories" that clients tell themselves in order

to establish, or maintain, meaning in their lives. The role of the therapist is not only that of an engaged listener but also of "attendant" (the original meaning of therapist) in that he or she is also involved in the explication of the client narrative via various forms of clarificatory and challenging input. It is, therefore, the very relationship that develops between therapist and client that is the central constituent of the therapeutic enterprise. (pp. 1-2)

Intervention, as we see it, is an attempt to explore the multiple ways in which partners caught up in intimate violence make sense of their lives. The spouses' narratives of violence can be visualized in terms of the figure-ground metaphor (Valle & King, 1978). We can therefore view the violence as the background to their life or vice versa. Our purpose is to help people to possess their experiences and their life stories in a manner that will enable them to defuse the violence and create another scenario—this time, violence free. The alternative will already incorporate the assumption of responsibility for choices made. In putting the new story together, one should emphasize the understanding of the other's subjectivity rather than treating the other as an "object." The professional functions here as catalyst and frames the process. By so doing, he or she helps clients acquire enough security to be able to take a reflective stance toward the meanings developed in the course of living in violence. It is expected that the sense of security derived from the helping situation can serve as a shock absorber when the couple realizes the full implications of the past choices as well as the changes pertaining to considering alternative options.

Our method of intervention draws on more than 10 years of research and practice in the area of intimate violence. It draws on a variety of concepts discussed in previous chapters and is offered as a general orientation to be further developed and applied under specific practice circumstances.

Making the Process of Meaning Construction Explicit

When acts of violence are incorporated into a way of life, what would seem to an observer as horrible and intolerable comes to be taken for granted by the parties involved. Intervention is directed toward the discovery of the horror of violence, the analysis of its taken-for-grantedness.

The process of intervention has to put the client in touch with the edifice of meanings underlying his or her everyday world of things and feelings. Let us illustrate this process by examining the violent event. Men and women typically have a pretty clear idea of how the violent event evolved. More often than not, each one regards the other as the instigator and oneself as having been dragged in. Moreover, each party almost invariably forms a rigid grid of categories that are used to assign any form of the partner's behavior a so-called archetype. Thus, whether she answers back or keeps quiet, she is branded "provocative." Or from her viewpoint of a person living underground, so to speak (there being so much to hide), the most innocuous (to us) items of information (today, she baked a cake) are still rated top secret.

One productive method of delineating the mechanism operating in the mind of a violent man who in effect disowns his violence is this: The wickedness and horror of it are projected on her, the instigator. She is not only the vicious cause but is doubly diabolical since he acts in the open and she acts covertly. (Notice the correspondence to her so-called secret life.)

The practitioner ought to resist the temptation to act as arbitrator or detective with regard to the parties' versions, lest he or she lose the special position as one who can show the couple the way out of their impasse. The crucial move, rather, is to penetrate through the presented narratives to form a comprehensive view of the interactive patterns that trigger violence and serve to incorporate it into their daily life.

One way of tackling this task is to draw the spouses' attention to their specific way of dealing with quotidian matters, such as parenting, money management, allocation of household chores, and so forth. This could be the beginning of a new and fruitful dialogue.

The Intersubjective Nature of Interpersonal Encounters

Our intervention model is based on the assumption that the meaning we give to our existence in the world with others is intersubjective (Becker, 1992; Duck, 1994; Guidano, 1995; Laing, 1960). We don't infer the other's subjectivity from observing his or her behavior, we rather read the behavior as manifestation of a subjectivity.

Thus, accounts chosen by the parties often support an implicit agreement that they are a normal couple and that violence is a rare and negligible occurrence between them. The defining of a victim or a perpetrator and what constitutes violence is not a single-handed enterprise but rather the result of collaboration between intimates. Such definitions are the outcome of negotiation, conflict, and power struggles. For example, pushing or shoving may be defined by the man as the means of avoiding "real" violence and therefore will not only be characterized by him as nonviolent but will be seen as a preventive measure. The woman, however, may reject his definition and eventually persuade him that it was indeed violence. The result may be a shared reality, wherein the man accepts that his behavior was too aggressive. They may end up compromising that there was no violent intent attached to the pushing. Subsequently, they might even come to agree that in general, an act without violent intent is not "really" violent.

The professional strives toward a dialogue between the parties based on mutual recognition of the other's inner feelings rather than on viewing the other as a source of terror, fear, and manipulation. We must ask our clients persistently, "How does the other perceive what you say, do, feel? How do you understand his or her understanding? What are the potential gains or losses from accepting the other's way of feeling? We have shown in preceding chapters that the battered woman tends to regard the batterer as dangerous and weak at the same time. Thus, she interprets his violence as uncontrolled. Through intervention, we must enable her to reframe him as a person who acts based on decisions. Only such a position will allow for self-assertive communication. The man, in turn, views his partner as an aggressor who provokes and perpetuates his violence. There is a major gap between their perceptions that must be bridged if he is to become responsive to her needs while asserting his. By facilitating such intersubjective processes, professionals foster a reflective stance toward mutuality. It should be emphasized again that change in relationships can only be hoped for if there is a willingness to acknowledge the woman's inalienable right to her own different point of view.

The Need to Change the Language
in Order to Change People

To understand the unique culture and system of symbols of intimate violence, we need to address the language in which it is narrated. Because most violence is not witnessed by others, its experience is both conveyed and validated by language. As Efran, Lukens, and Lukens (1988) say, "Language is the one essential that such complex coordinations of action in a social community cannot do without and cally being conversations" (p. 32).

Without language, it is impossible to understand the other or even oneself. When you change the language, then you change the symbolic buildings blocks with which people create their worlds. To fully appreciate the clinical and therapeutic significance of language, we need to dwell briefly on several assumptions. Language is not only a symbol of objects or situations but the very condition of their existence for us. In other words, language determines the relation between symbols and thought processes, and as such, it has the power to shape both symbolic reality and its perception (Akillas & Efran, 1989; Palmer, 1969). Language has two seemingly contradictory functions: to serve as a ready "packaging" for conveying meaning but also to serve as a simple, sufficiently nuanced medium to describe the complex. For instance, a batterer said, "I came to the boiling point and hit her." On a superficial level, there is a description of a violent event here. The man was angry and beat his spouse. On a deeper level, a more complicated message is being conveyed: The actor provided an explanation of his behavior as well as a sequencing of its occurrence.

Words are not merely representative of reality but are reality itself, due to their prescriptive, organizing, framing, and actualizing power for behavior, thoughts, and emotions. They also serve as boundaries, in the sense that they demarcate what is included and excluded or what is real or unreal in a certain experience. For instance, many women reject the label "battered" because by accepting this characterization, they implicitly subscribe to the symbolic reality inherent in it, which is objectionable. Moreover, one language may have an integrative power because by its usage, it provides continuity and coherence to experiences that could seem fragmented through the prism of another language. For instance, talking about one's partner as being dangerous or out of control commits the speaker to being on guard perpetually, ready to defend herself from possible aggression at any time. Dangerousness also prescribes a certain set of behaviors, attitudes, and interpersonal distance. The inner reality, as we experience it, is essentially metaphorical (Romanyshyn, 1982). Therefore, metaphors constitute a powerful existential device by which the various functions of language come to dramatic expression. For instance, we have shown that if a perpetrator perceives his conflictual relationship with his partner as a war, his inner reality is one of a warrior. This way of seeing changes the rules of interaction so that, because the other is the enemy, offensive acts are conceived as defense.

Through intervention, we can help partners to develop an alternative linguistic structure that includes accounts and metaphors within which violence will be perceived as foreign and meaningless. To this end, professionals need to consciously map their client's linguistic structures so as to avoid being seduced by the power of the batterer's language. Following this, we can proceed to challenge their current linguistic framework by asking the batterer questions such as, "What would it be like if you didn't have to account for your violence?" or "What would it be like if you didn't expect your partner to account for your violence?" or "How would you depict your relationship if you didn't describe it as a 'war?'" Similarly, we could ask the woman, "What would you feel if you gave up the idea that your partner is not responsible for the violence?" or "What would it be like if you needed to give up the language of the loss of control for yourself or your partner?" This way, clients are made aware of the transformational power of their language.

Reconstructing the Client's Narratives

In previous parts of this book, we have described the various themes that partners living in violence deploy to organize their meaning system. These themes, arranged in a specific time sequence, constitute their narratives (Denzin, 1989; Ricoeur, 1979; Widdershoven, 1993). They are usually composed of two intertwined story threads: one of the violence and the other of their joint life. The integration of these into a historical context is essential, for it has an impact on what takes place in the actor's existential present. In the process of creating and re-creating meaning in their lives, people develop a coherent story line by injecting an adequate amount of causality and continuity (Linde, 1993). One's life story goes beyond one's inner experience, because it mirrors in the self the strategies used to communicate with others and claims to membership in social groups within a given sociohistorical context.

When the story of violence is told, the narrator needs to adjust various themes in his or her life to accommodate the violence. By the same token, when violence stops, the persons involved will need to alter their stories to make it plausible despite its cessation. The purpose of intervention is to examine the two versions and to show how they determine one another, thereby providing the actors with the components for an alternative narrative. The professional extracts the implicit structure of the narrative and makes it explicit to the client.

Questions such as "How does the person tell the story of the violence in the context of his life, and how does he or she tie it to his or her past and future?" and "How do partners living in violence negotiate a joint narrative, if there isn't one?" are part of this clarification process. For instance, finding out how violent events end or inquiring into the ways joint arrangements are formed concerning life together in violence is illuminating. A diachronic perspective is acquired by probing into changes over time on such topics as these: "Did the ways in which you make up change as time passed?" or "How would you tell the story of violence 10 years from now?" It is important to show participants that they are active in choosing their narratives and to awaken them to the hidden benefits of telling the story one way rather than another. This will bring home to the couple that they are active in choosing their narratives. A thorough examination of its structure and content will hopefully lead to the understanding that alternative narratives are needed.

Violence as a Way of Life
Rather Than a Symptom

Intimate violence creates an existential situation that becomes all-encompassing and affects identities, relationships, and roles, as well as the perception of time, places, and other people. It has a sui-generis quality, with a life of its own, which colors and dictates the way of being in the world. One is violent over and above being anything else, and violence is both the cause and the consequence of most existential experiences. One is not a partner or a father but a violent partner and father. Violence creates a field of experience of the self and of others that is imbued with attempts to retrieve something felt to be lost (Denzin, 1984): loosing yet more in the process of attempting to regain, feeling guilt and shame for the violence, searching for ways to justify it, attempting to avoid its impact on other aspects of life, using face-saving tactics to shield the social identity of victim or the perpetrator, striving to save the family unit in spite of the violence, and trying to compensate for the violence. These processes are consuming and drain most of the participants' resources. When the contents of the couplehood consists mainly of struggle, denial and deceit, and loss of security and the sense of hearth and home base, spouses become strangers in their own home. Furthermore, violence has a self-desensitizing effect by which the actors' tolerance of violence increases, and their definition changes of what is violent and what is not. Parallel to such

processes, is an increased tendency toward control and power struggles. In such a changed interpersonal context, partners may collude in
redefining violent and nonviolent acts as two separate paths and survive within this reconstructed reality.

Recognizing this state of affairs implies that intervention is
directed to changing the total worldview of people who live in violence rather than altering some of their specific behaviors, emotions,
or cognitive structures. It centers on developing consciousness of the
ways in which their entire existential experience has been affected by
violence rather than highlighting some of its specific aspects. The key
questions around which intervention centers are, "How did violence
change you as a person?" "How did it change your way of being in the
world?" "How did it change your perceptions and relationships with
others?" "How did it change your attitudes and values?" Specific
intervention goals and techniques need to be integrated within these
broad questions as part of an ongoing dialogue, which may have many
confrontational and tactical elements with both the perpetrator and
the survivor.

Intimate Violence as a Social Problem and
Intervention as Part of Its Social Construction

Violence against women should be treated in its social, historical,
political, and institutional contexts (Dobash & Dobash, 1990). These
parameters need to be taken into account in any specific intervention
situation. Such an approach is particularly significant in the light of
the historical denial and neglect of the sociocultural roots of the problem, its prevalence, and its influence on the quality of life of partners
from different social and ethnic subcultures. Selective inattention to
some of the broader contextual variables is often expressed by the tendency of many professionals to overlook the violence that is conspicu-
ous among middle-class clients and to place more emphasis on family
integrity and on privacy than on safety and women's rights, and so
forth. On the other hand, violence is often overcontextualized,
trivialized, and relegated to pathology or problematic interpersonal
dynamics, to the utter neglect of it being a way to control, terrorize,
and intimidate women. It is important to note that such interpretations have a bearing on the client's already existing inclination to minimize or deny the problem altogether (Aldarondo & Straus, 1994;
Gondolf, 1993; Walker, 1979). Such a therapeutic attitude leads
to victim blaming and to focusing on the children rather than on

their mother as objects of abuse. It also makes the woman out to be a coabuser, pathologizing her continuous or intermittent presence or accusing her of leaving. An overall defeatist attitude preventing the overcoming of violence is thereby rendered self-perpetuating (e.g., Eisikovits & Buchbinder, 1996; Mullender, 1996). A series of misapplied professional principles and values reinforce these misguided tendencies. For instance, the idea that professionals should be neutral, that they should accept clients as they are, be nondirective, expect the clients to initiate discussion about their problems, search for problems in the relationship and not in one or the other party, focus on communication, collect information from both partners and judge their accuracy; all of these tend to make the treatment part of the problem rather than part of the solution (e.g., Aldarondo & Straus, 1994; Harway & Hansen, 1993).

In every intervention, there is potential for either psychological reductionism or for a broader social contextual approach that takes into account the pitfalls previously mentioned. The lesson of social constructionism is that we should concentrate on the client's narratives while asking questions such as "What are the social and political circumstances that conditioned the client's memory as he or she tried to cope with violence?" or "How did their previous experiences with various official and unofficial help and other interlocutors affect their narratives?" or "Is the woman's story adapted to social desirability and to pressure arising from a given sociopolitical situation?" or "Did the man draw additional power and control from the way he presented the story of violence and manipulated the professional reaction to it?" Thus, it is preferable that every treatment situation be viewed as a renewed social construction in which the worker is an integral part.

Intervention in Domestic Violence
Always Value Based

Expectations of making intervention "scientific" in recent years were associated with attempts to dissociate the process from its value context (Sato, 1991). The empirically based practice movement, for instance, emphasized the way we can measure "what works in intervention"—in the best positivistic tradition. This implied that measurement, as well as intervention, should be as objective and value free as possible. Whereas such an approach does not preclude ethical concerns, it views them as marginal. In contrast to this approach, we affirm a conception of practice that is primarily a value-based, ethical

enterprise. Empirical measurement is important, but it should be performed while taking into account that practice itself is a process of
social construction (Loewenberg & Dolgoff, 1996).

Some interventions are problematic from an ethical standpoint,
yet they are still carried out. For instance, a professional may suggest
to a survivor to involve the police, knowing the potentially adverse
consequences of such a step for the client and family. Also, the decision concerning a given path of intervention may lead to severe difficulties in the client-professional relationship. For instance, most
violent men refuse to define themselves as such, and when confronted
with the label, they tend to develop animosity to the point of dropping
out of treatment. Similarly, many women recognize the existence of
difficulties in their married life without acknowledging the presence
of violence as the organizing factor in their marriage; hence, the
required focus of the intervention is missing. When such a focus is suggested, this usually leads to alienation from the professional and to
rejection of the intervention. A conflict may arise between principles
underlying intervention and values stemming from specific cultural
and social needs. For instance, our clinical practices often confronted
us with situations where women chose couple intervention just
because they wanted to continue the marriage out of cultural constraints or out of economic necessity. In certain cultural and ethnic
groups (e.g., Muslims or Orthodox Jews), we cannot measure the
willingness or unwillingness to terminate the marriage by Western
standards, because divorce is seen as exacting a higher social price
than the violence itself.

Given the foregoing, professionals must clarify their own value
systems to themselves and their clients. The value context of clients
should also be explored, because many are not aware of or able to
articulate their assumed stands, but they invariably act on them. This
kind of exploration leads to questions such as, How can the worker
bridge possible gaps between client rights and sociocultural expectations? How can workers prioritize between client needs, agency
needs, and worker accountability when these are inconsistent? Whose
subjective perception (the woman's, the man's, or the worker's) will
have primacy in the definition of the situation? Who is the client: the
woman, the man, the couple, the entire family? What are the ethical
implications of making choices as to the identity of the client? These
illustrations indicate the importance of making the values underlying
intervention and professional decisions explicit and using them
actively in professional encounters.

Focusing on Emotions in Violence

In various parts of this book, we have shown how intimate violence involves a web of emotions that both lead to, and result from, violence. We have similarly demonstrated that positive and negative emotions (e.g., love and guilt) feed on each other and create a dynamic balance. They are powerful guidelines for action, which attempt to bridge between the world as it is and the one we want it to be. Emotions are always directed to intentional objects, including oneself and the other. Being close to another person is tantamount to having that person's emotional makeup as a constituent of one's subjective core.

The purpose of the intervention is to foster a reflective stance toward the emotions leading to a concrete sense that change is possible. This can be done by facilitating the verbalization of emotional experiences (Greenberg & Pascual-Leone, 1997). The process consists of several interlocking therapeutic acts: First, we single out a specific feeling that seems central to the client and proceed to discuss the associated words, bodily sensations, thoughts, and their contexts. Thereby, we help the clients toward insight into their inner logic. For instance, guilt may be associated with conflict between taking and rejecting responsibility; the creation of a hostile world is not fully comprehensible to the client, in most cases. Second, we attempt to increase the client's awareness of other emotions, related to the one under scrutiny, that may be masked by it. For instance, love may mask anger toward the partner as well as masking a series of negative emotions toward oneself, such as guilt and shame. It may also mask a sense of superiority over one's partner. We may then be able to show that love—as a mask—cannot really compensate for violence. Third, we need to examine the broader script of which the identified emotions are but a part. By so doing, we are able to tie them to behavior, relationships, and interpretations along a time axis. For instance, we have shown that love and guilt may create an illusory world that traps the partners in a ritual of inauthenticity but also becomes their rigid blueprint for coping with violence. Fourth, we attempt to move with the clients toward the development of alternative scripts. For instance, we try to get the clients to feel "sheer guilt" for their violence, without recourse to explanations that are both self-exonerating and accusatory (i.e., ways of entrapping the other in their own guilt). The scripts direct clients toward reconstructing their experience of intimacy, security, and mutual acceptance.

Therapy and Social Control as
Basic Elements of Intervention

Professional intervention in intimate violence needs to address the question of locating specific professional activities along a continuum, with social control at one end and therapy at the other (Goldner, 1992). This has also been conceptualized at times as the dilemma of compassion versus control (Mederer & Gelles, 1989). Such a locating process involves the definition of the situation as either criminal or clinical. If the situation is defined as one of control, the boundaries of the treatment situation are irrelevant, because social measures are necessary to restrain the criminal. The professional becomes one of several control agents performing this social function. On the other hand, if the situation is defined as therapeutic, it will supposedly remain within the confines of treatment, though keeping the boundary with the opposite pole will become a major issue. Helping professionals are socialized to regard themselves as altruists whose ideal is to help rather than restrain. Given this, there is a tendency among helping professionals to exaggerate the gap between the two extremes. This in turn gives clients the impression that most helping professionals are not control agents at all. Confusion is caused by the misconception that helping professionals are not part of the same power structure that controls all deviance—from mental illness to crime (Goldner, 1992). It also creates a fictitious hierarchy of interventions based on the extent to which they are more or less therapylike. Regarded by workers in this way, the therapeutic session seems to gain magical powers and thereby becomes the main source of hope for any change to take place. Conversely, conceptualizing intervention as control only may also have negative consequences. It may create the fantasy that change may be imposed. It can also minimize dialogue and all independent decision and choice by the parties.

The therapy-versus-control dilemmas are further complicated by the divergent expectations the partners attach to the therapeutic situation. Both consider outside intervention in their lives as a major turning point, but the perceptions and expectations they hold in common end here. The man comes (or more often is brought) to intervention due to his wish to keep the couple an autonomous unit; he wishes to keep his independence, so he views therapy as an intrusion on his freedom; he tends to transfer responsibility to the partner or, at best, to share it; he expects a rational and cognitive approach; he wants the therapist's unreserved acceptance of his version while keeping a comfortable interpersonal distance from him or her. When his narrative is not fully endorsed, he feels besieged. Outside intervention is perceived as questioning his normality identity, his power position, and his family life as a whole. The woman, by contrast, is far more inviting of the professional to enter the boundaries of the relationship. She lays full responsibility on her husband and expects unconditional acceptance of her version. She expects emotional commitment and closeness in her relationship with the therapist. When her narrative is doubted, she feels rejected and disillusioned. Just like her partner, she is also struggling to maintain her self-perception as a normal person.

Our method of intervention proposes a framework that combines both control and therapy. It must consider the multiple ways in which a problem may be constructed, framed, and presented by participants. For instance, we need to convey the message that intimate violence has legal consequences and involves legal responsibility. At the same time, we offer our professional help in addition to, rather than instead of, legally based social control. We explicitly present ourselves as part of a continuum of interventions. Thus, as part of our contract, we make it clear to the husband that repeated violence will not remain within the therapeutic boundaries. We further clarify to the man that we will use coercion to expose him to and keep him in treatment.

The Need to Bridge Between Violence and Gender Relationships

Among those who work with survivors and perpetrators of intimate violence, there is a consensus that intimate violence cannot be dissociated from the asymmetric power relations between the genders. Feminist theoreticians and practitioners have emphasized the connection between the unequal power distribution in society and the family and have explained the occurrence of violence as an expression thereof. Women's attempts to question the justice of the status quo concerning power relations are usually perceived by men as a threat to their hegemony and social privilege (e.g., Yllö, 1993). However, attempts to implement these assumptions in daily practice are hampered by a series of complications. These need further elaboration. First, one cannot assume that gender equality or inequality is an issue for all or most men or women. A gap between the perceptions of professionals and clients in this area may lead to ineffective communication. Second, even where there is awareness of the specific issue of gender inequality, it is so much taken for granted that it has little explanatory power in regarding the client's experience. Third, the majority of clients we have encountered have not been fully aware of the overriding impact of gender on their everyday lives. Taken-for-grantedness coupled with the minimization of the impact of gender blur the connection between power-based gender asymmetry and intimate violence. To all of this should be added the threat involved in making the connection between gender and violence explicit. This threat is manifested in both partners' experience in a variety of ways: The battered woman's recognition of the connection involves coping with violence as well as with belonging to the oppressed class. This often leads to a basic sense of hopelessness arising from the idea that even if violence should stop at some point, the relief will be only temporary, because her victim identity is socially conditioned and shaped by large forces beyond her interpersonal life. Similarly, the man who makes the explicit link between gender and violence will come to the realization that he is both an aggressor and a member of the oppressors' class. People feel better equipped and competent to manage an interpersonal conflict than a class struggle. On the whole, our experience with clients has shown that although being a representative of a class may sometimes add to one's strength, it is too much of a load for most clients and leads to a sense of depersonalization and distance from both the problem and the partner. Even if we assume that most professionals are aware of the connection between gender relations and violence, they still face a major dilemma. They have to achieve neutrality and avoid a judgmental approach toward their client's sociocultural attitudes and values while advocating that focusing on the violence alone will lead to mere localized and temporary results. Focusing on the violence will leave the social structural causes of violence intact.

Taking this into account, our intervention scheme is guided by several complex messages: First, we believe that a connection between intimate violence and gender relations must be an explicitly stated focus of intervention with clients. At the same time, we should take into account that gender socialization limits the flexibility of both men and women in their attempts to make changes in their lives. An ongoing dialogue concerning gender attitudes, values, and socialization processes enables clients to experience the considerable impact of gender on most aspects of their daily lives. The influence of gender on violent conflicts is a good example. For instance, the choice of conflictual topics is gender related. A man may feel that it is his right to know and control his wife's whereabouts and space, whereas the woman may resist it. A woman may feel that it is her prerogative to educate the children, but her husband may try to interfere. By analyzing such seemingly isolated and extreme cases, we may point out to our clients the metastructures and rules governing such interactions and their gender character. We present a hierarchy of changes required to stop violence to the clients and frame such metastructures as top priorities, given their considerable destructive power. Once partners realize the impact of gender in their life, a sense of a total uprooting of previously existing meanings may be experienced (Marris, 1980). Intensive guidance for the development of an alternative meaning system, in which there is no place for violence, is expected from professionals.

The Polarity Between Paternalism and Self-Determination in the Treatment Relationship

Underlying the overall client-worker relationships is a socially constructed power differential based on role expectations and behaviors, assumed knowledge gaps, and power to help. This is further exacerbated in the situations of violence in which imminent danger and the need to predict, prevent, and protect are acute. Most professionals working with survivors of violence feel responsible for their clients' well-being but above all, for their survival. Such dramatic elements enhance the paternalistic tendency inherent in the helping situation. On the other hand, pointing out opportunities for self-determination are at the heart of good professional practice. Professionals working in intimate violence may often come to the conclusion that self-determination is not an option when clients' lives are at high risk or when their behavior instigates the violence. The professional is thus faced with several sets of dilemmas: How much of the focus and goals of treatment should be imposed by him or her and how far should he or she allow clients to self-determine these? This is critical in the light of clinical and research evidence showing that both husband and wife tend to develop a variety of strategies to cope with and live with the violence. These include denial, forgetfulness, minimization, reframing, and enlisting economic or other extrinsic circumstances (e.g., Bograd, 1988; Hyden, 1994), all of which may defocus the intervention process and cause the violence itself to be side-stepped. These strategies are not specific to men, for it has been found that women tend to use more accounts and justifications to avoid dealing directly with violence than men do (Eisikovits, Goldblatt, & Winstok, 1999). However, at times, by focusing on violence, we may accelerate the breakdown of the existing defenses without offering an alternative. This could lead to more violence or to dropping out of treatment.

A related dilemma centers around the extent to which the worker should accept the rhythm of the client or serve as a catalyst in enhancing the progress toward specific goals to be attained. Help seeking is a complex process of weighing the help, the support, and the freedom acquired through the intervention against the client's losses and costs. The timetable chosen for confronting the partner in the helping process, involving outside agents in the family, encouraging formal complaints and thus raising doubts concerning loyalty, leaving the relationship, and so forth, may all be critical decisions. If not timed properly, they may lead to an escalation of rather than a diminishing of violence. Freedom from violence may involve actions such as leaving or separating, which may be desirable from the worker's point of view but not feasible for the client at a given point in time.

It is suggested that an intervention use the clients' subjective perceptions of the situation and respect their decisions as part of the process of strengthening as baseline (Register, 1993). Homogenization, oversimplification, and perception of the women as deviant when she makes decisions contrary to professional scripts should be avoided (Baker, 1997; Loseke & Cahill, 1984). However, workers should be quite explicit about their constraints and clearly spell out their positions concerning nonnegotiable topics. The most obvious of such constraints are legal (as in cases of child abuse) or when the worker believes that the woman is in an actual life-threatening situation. It would be easiest to solve the dilemma by denying paternalism altogether. However, in everyday life, practitioners are faced with situations in which self-determination cannot be achieved when dealing with clients whose lives are being threatened or are unable to self-determine themselves at the desired pace. Thus, we return to our earlier suggestion of a flexible continuum along which we can place various treatment situations as lending themselves to greater or less self-determination.

Perpetrator's Responsibility Versus Shared Responsibility for Violence Individualized and Contextualized

The issue of taking responsibility for the violence is critical in all modes of intervention. Professional reactions to the issue of responsibility can be broadly conceptualized along a continuum at one end of which are those who maintain that perpetrators are exclusively responsible and at the other, those who claim that violence is the result of interactive and mutual inputs (Giles-Simes, 1983; Hansen, 1993; Margolin & Burman, 1993). A clear-cut position on this issue is harder to formulate than one may suppose. First, the issue of responsibility hangs on our paradigm of choice concerning causality. In a paradigm based on linear causality, one may take the clear position that responsibility is focused and lies with the perpetrator. Isolating violence from other aspects of joint life confines the possibilities available to intervention to a specific, narrow region that may provide the batterer with ready excuses. Furthermore, the concept of exclusive responsibility relentlessly assigns very definite roles, which mates living in violence are loath to acquiescence to. Men tend to deny being perpetrators, or at least they make attempts to persuade their interlocutor that there is more to them than being just that. Women seldom accept the role of victim because it weakens them, and they often prefer a shared responsibility and guilt to a sense of total powerlessness and loss of control over their lives. It often happens in intervention that one of the partners is willing to take responsibility for a specific occurrence but is quite unwilling to see it as characteristic behavior. In sum, a hasty assignment of responsibility that does not take into account the foregoing points may have a fragmentizing effect and destroy the clients' experience unrecognizably.

How can the professional be clear and unequivocal about the issue of responsibility while taking into account the aforementioned complexities? We found it useful to work with clients individually and jointly to understand the relevant social and psychological constructions of responsibility while taking full account of their subjective perspectives. At the same time, we suggest focusing on choices made by individuals within the constraint of their perceptions and interpretations. We have to make them see the influences these interpretations have on the way they envision their options, constantly pointing out that choice is inevitable. Alternative choices can then be suggested, against a background of a plurality of interpretations. The use of violence is thereby framed as an unfortunate choice that cannot be presented as exclusive, inevitable, or morally justifiable. Last, by making violence a matter of choice, we emphasize to the perpetrator that he does have control over his violent acts and to the survivor that she can choose her way of reacting to it.

Addressing the Victim or the Survivor,
the Violent Man or the Man Who
Committed Violent Acts

The use of this terminology reaches beyond the labels themselves, as it implies personal, social, and public identities with far-reaching implications as to societal reactions in general and intervention approaches in particular. How do we perceive the clients for whom violence is a way of life, at various points in the intervention process? Has involvement in violence set participants apart and made them forever different from those of us who don't experience it in our lives? Should women who have been abused be perceived as victims or survivors? Being a victim implies passivity, weakness, and helplessness. Victims are usually described as having defective personalities, as dependent on others, and without control over their lives (Browne, 1991). In general, they are cast in a negative social role. On the other hand, victims gain attention and high priority; they are seen as needy and given help within an empathic atmosphere. At times, the victim role for battered women is like a rest area in which they temporarily place themselves to gather strength for coping with violence.

Survivors are perceived as strong, vital, and competent persons who are able to cope, actively seek help, and make choices concerning priorities. When battered women are presented as survivors, their strength is emphasized by the suggestion of surviving against all odds in a hostile and male-controlled environment (Profitt, 1996). The image of the survivor, however, raises high expectations of an aptitude for coping, but it also desensitizes the terrible suffering caused by violence. Battered women have traditionally been perceived as victims and only more recently as survivors (Bowker, 1993; Gondolf & Fisher, 1988).

Men who beat their spouses have rarely been portrayed as victims, and when so described, they were usually presented as prey to their own tempers or impulses. Their standard public image has been that of aggressors. As such, they were more often deemed "violent men" than "men who committed violent acts." Their social identity emphasized habitual use of force to achieve their goals and their dominance over women. This was associated with low self-esteem, suppressed emotions, and explosiveness. Such social and psychological characteristics joined together in creating the image of the man who attacks and should be considered dangerous. The image of the man who has committed violent acts is less appealing because of its relative complexity and because it goes against the grain of the political correctness in a feminist-inspired society trying to rid itself of a long-standing patriarchal tradition and collective guilt associated with it. Indeed, there are genuine dangers inherent in the concept of a man who acted violently and still claims a share in humanity. Such a conception could easily be misused to condone violence and blur the demarcation between victim and perpetrator, as many men try to do, particularly in therapeutic situations.

Whereas on the prescriptive level, we embrace the metaphor of survivors and its connotations as a key concept in approaching battered women, we believe that in actual practice, a judicious flexibility is required in applying the notions of "victims" and "survivors." At various stages of working with battered women, one should allow for temporary self-definitions and possible movement between these. We should always maintain realistic expectations concerning what the battered woman can handle at different stages of her coping with the violence and its aftermath. As for the batterers, we prefer the use of the term "men who committed violent acts." This option focuses attention on their violence while at the same time, enabling work with the rest of their humanness. However, the distinction between those two categories is conceptually problematic, because for the clinician, the man sitting before him is a man who has lived a violent way of life, hence his entire subjectivity is contaminated by violence. The point is, however, that for didactical and therapeutic purposes, approaching the man as possessing human qualities over and above his violence may function as a self-fulfilling prophecy facilitating improvement. Change requires a total transformation or identity conversion, which would entail not only a change in behavior but also in values, beliefs, lifestyles, priorities, and life goals. Thus, we should expect a slow and cumbersome process in which the therapist should continuously highlight the distinction between support for the person and condemnation of the violent acts.

The Assessment as the Primary Script
of the Therapist

Professionals are involved in constantly assessing their clients. Whether it is done systematically as part of a preconceived protocol or intuitively and freely, it is highly significant, as it determines the script by which the act, the actors, and their context will be constructed.

When such a script is formed, it is as if it were carved in stone, a stigma that makes the self-fulfilling prophecy inescapable. Although we recognize that modern assessment is expected to be dynamic, our clinical experience shows that changes can mostly be expected within the initial script rather than in the script itself. When doing assessment, professionals are faced initially with two major problems: First, battering takes place in places and situations that do not lend themselves to direct observation. Second, the reliability of the assessment depends on the degree of correspondence between the various versions (Tolman, 1992). Full correspondence is rare, as partners are in conflict, and their constructions are divergent concerning what took place, as well as why and how. Reporting is often influenced by emotions such as fear, guilt, shame, and loyalty, as well as concern for the possible influence of outside interference in the clients' lives on the part of various control agents. Divergent cultural and social attitudes as well as cost-benefit considerations also affect reporting. Can practitioners live with different versions without succumbing to the temptation to try to find out "the true" version? One major goal of the assessment of cohabiting couples who have experienced violence is to create a dialogue concerning violence. To this end, the existence of multiple perspectives may be functional. The practitioners will use these versions to create their own professional script that is based on the state of the art in the field and personal knowledge, as well as clients' versions. To accomplish a comprehensive assessment of client problems, the following information will prove to be useful:

> Kinds of violence that took place over time, including physical, sexual, and psychological, as well as destruction of property (The client's estimation of the chances of repeated violence ought to be considered.)
>
> Violent behavior outside the family and examination of a possible history of criminal violence
>
> History and present use of drugs and alcohol
>
> History of psychiatric treatment or hospitalizations
>
> Possible posttraumatic stress disorder symptoms
>
> Causes and motivations for violence
>
> Partners' awareness concerning the pernicious effect of violence on the children
>
> Partners' goals for the future
>
> Communicative competence of partners
>
> Material resources available to the partners
>
> Attitudes toward agents of social intervention

The Need to Assess
the Degree of Danger

Partners living in violence view themselves as living in danger to some degree. This may be either tactical or genuine, but under no circumstance can it be ignored. For instance, if a man chooses to behave in a way that suggests that he is dangerous, then he is in fact dangerous, by the behavioral consequences of his constructions. Thus, any intervention should pay special attention to assessing dangerousness and the possibility of escalation to high-risk violence (Straus, 1996). This should be given priority as both a practical and an ethical concern. On the practical level, we are familiar with a series of life-threatening factors that should be assessed on an ongoing basis. These are (a) a history of repeated violence, including forced sex; (b) threats or fantasies of killing or committing suicide; (c) availability of a weapon and use of a weapon or threats to use one; (d) extreme expressions of possessiveness or jealousy associated with placing the partner at the center of the person's life and attempts to control the other's movements; (e) violence and threats at times of separation and loss; (f) willingness to take risks with little or no concern for the personal, social, and legal consequences; (g) severe depression and other psychological problems; (h) repeated use of alcohol and drugs; (i) child abuse at present and a history of being abused as a child; (j) violence toward animals; and (k) severe and repeated destruction of property (Campbell, 1995; Straus,1996). The more of these risk factors present, the greater the danger. Once these risk factors are identified, we have the legal, ethical, and professional obligation to act immediately. Action should be guided by the principle of warning and protecting. Warning includes counseling the potential victim as to the specific risky situations in her life and signs for recognizing them. A safety plan, which should always be part of working with battered women, becomes critical and should be systematically rehearsed in cases of severe danger. It includes uncovering cues of violence, finding an escape route, preparing support systems that can help and calling for help or protection, and learning about sources of help and support available in the community (Gondolf, 1998). Protecting also means that practitioners who are aware of immediate danger should call the police and help prepare a secure environment for the woman, such as a shelter or a safe home. In cases of extreme danger, the control function of professionals supersedes their helping function.

Method of Intervention: Individual
Rather Than Couple Based

Initially, intervention focuses on the individual partners. This is related to our belief that violence has created a field of experience, imbued with alienation and apartness, that cannot be readily bridged in the presence of both sides. The content of the universe they inhabit is conflictual and contradictory. The violence damages the identities of the partners involved, and the problems in the relationship are the consequences rather than the causes of violence. Also, the different narratives recounted by partners cannot be bridged in the initial stage of the intervention. Focusing on individuals is also important because it allows each partner to temper the extreme emotional outbursts occasioned by the situation. Separation allows one to focus on individual interpretations and meanings without having to seek validation from the other partner, which is likely to be problematic at this point.

Couple therapy with partners involved in intimate violence is controversial (Bograd, 1984; Edleson & Tolman, 1992; Hansen, 1993; Margolin & Burman, 1993; Trute, 1998; Walker, 1994). It has been argued that couple therapy may place the woman in danger and may imply that she shares responsibility for the occurrence and resolution of the violence. The man may interpret the therapeutic situation in a manner that may provide him with justification for his violence. The woman may fear to report violence in joint sessions and focus on her need to defend herself rather than be authentically involved in the process. Moreover, the couple therapy situation may hamper the process of enhancing the battered woman's strength because this often needs to be done by working through her anger and using it as a catalyst toward empowerment. The partner's presence may become a barrier to the expression of her anger.

Couple therapy has often been criticized because of sexist attitudes expressed in tendencies of therapists to form coalitions with the man. When this happens, it enables the man to continuously deny the patriarchal power structure in the family. Therapists' tendencies to keep the family intact may be stigmatizing for those women who do not fit the normative mold concerning family structure. In individual sessions, both partners might be able to build trust toward the therapist, for their experiences so far have oversensitized them to danger and, in particular, the hazards of misplaced trust (Walker, 1994).

Men also start from a position of suspicion, particularly if coerced into treatment, which is often the case. They are vulnerable owing to their weakened identity and experience of loss. In most cases, they believe that the world is against them and that social control agents threaten the integrity of their families. Overcoming such initial fears through separate treatment may facilitate willingness for change (Gauthier & Levendosky, 1996). Whereas we strongly suggest that intervention should begin with partners as individuals, we find that for most partners, couplehood is important and becomes more so when besieged by violence. Thus, we explicitly state to partners that violence has created a gap between them, on all levels of experience, which cannot be faced by them together. But at the same time, we convey that we fully appreciate that they are struggling with their couplehood, and we will help them work together when the time is ripe.

Concluding Remarks

Professionals working with clients in intimate violence need to prepare themselves for a lengthy, highly complex, and seldom rewarding journey. When we first entered this field, we felt the pressure to provide quick remedies for pressing problems. As many others have, we too attempted to carve out an image of intimate violence that could be contained by mastering the techniques of anger management, cognitive restructuring, time out, anger logs, assertiveness training, and the like. We invested ourselves in advocating on behalf of battered women and for coercive therapy for their partners and persuaded them to stay away from their violent partners as much as possible. We drew satisfaction from the lowered rates of physical violence and made this the measure of our success. In time, we became less optimistic but wiser. Our research and practice experience moved us from mastering the techniques to understanding the complexities involved in our work.

In this chapter, we have attempted to propose guidelines for professional action with people living in intimate violence. The parameters we have used address issues concerning society, the therapist, and clients, as well as the dimensions of problem and context. Throughout our analysis, we have highlighted what to us seemed critical junctures and optimal intervention.

10

Postscript
The End Is the Beginning

When we set out to write this book, we hoped to draw the reader, if only temporarily, into the world of intimate violence, offering him or her the inside view. We tried to make the most of the fact that the closest you can get is the narrative recounted by the participants and our own understandings of their interpretations. We hope we were able to engage the reader in our dialogue with those who have lived in violence and have survived to tell the tale. In joining this dialogue, the reader has presumably formed his or her own "construction." It would be most rewarding if our independently minded readers stayed with us despite the differences and negotiated with us for yet a better choice.

We both come from a professional and academic tradition that looks for trouble. Human service professions often seem to think along the lines intimated by Tolstoy in *Anna Karenina,* namely that "happy families are all alike; every unhappy family is unhappy in its own way." Perhaps for this reason, grief has been researched more than satisfaction, pain and loss more than happiness, helplessness more than strength, wars more than peace, and violence more than nonviolence. It would do us no injustice to state that our choice to study intimate violence was rooted in similar motivations. We can only say that the focus of this book was not the striking hand alone, not the violent event alone. Rather, we have attempted to analyze how

163

couplehood survives intimate violence, how it is maintained, and what the dynamics are of living together with violence. By shedding light on the couplehood rather than on violence alone, we hope we were able to identify the light that may come after the darkness; love that may substitute for pain, hate, and indifference; the stroking hand that may substitute for the striking hand. However, only acquiring an understanding of the meaning structures and social scripts leading to violence will not do. Insights into moments of light and strength are no less important, because that's where the hope is hidden. Although there is a relatively large body of knowledge about loving and happy families, its interpretive understanding is limited. It is critical to examine how violence-free couplehood is experienced and constructed, what its dynamics, rules, and scripts are. If truth is a cultural construction resulting from social relationships, and if membership in specific subcultures generates differential perceptions of truth and lies, rights and wrongs, the cultural context that allows such realities to blossom needs to become an additional focus of inquiry. To this end, we would need to examine the social structures as well as the historical and cultural roots that generate specific sets of relationships and modes of negotiating that make for a violent or a nonviolent script. How do they evolve? What is the specific process by which cultural understandings are developed? How does aggression, conflict, and resistance, or alternatively, cooperation, acceptance, and agreement, grow within a set of relationships? Once we understand the positive scripts and their underlying cultural context, we could attempt to see what stops them from penetrating the world of intimate violence.

The book has attempted to address the question of how violent couplehood is possible. But what is more important to us is not whether this question has been fully answered but rather the broader one of whether the gains from this kind of journey into the complexities of life in the shadow of violence can affect the broader social discourse about intimate violence. Along these lines, we ask what the potential gains might be from understanding that we are involved in an ongoing creation of sociocutural scripts dependent on specific rules of the social dance. The hope is enfolded in the potential insights acquired from such an understanding: The script can be changed. The more we expose ourselves to as many cultural voices as possible, the more we can escape from the deterministic power of one voice that mesmerizes our deeds and be open to ongoing involvement in dialogues and multilogues toward accepting multiple social scripts and constructions of reality. The hope to avoid traps and identify desired paths depends on our ability to doubt what is perceived as objective and absolute truth.

Perhaps this book, which deals with the painful scars of couplehood in violence, suffering and terror, validates Sartre's statement, in his play *No Exit,* that "hell is other people." But this focus on hell should not mean that paradise has been lost sight of. In fact, one of the central messages we hope to convey is the need to search for the roads leading to it.

References

Akillas, E., & Efran, J. (1989). Internal conflict, language and metaphor: Implications for psychotherapy. *Journal of Contemporary Psychotherapy, 19,* 149-159.

Aldarondo, E., & Straus, M. A. (1994). Screening for physical violence in couple therapy: Methodological, practical and ethical consideration. *Family Process, 33,* 425-439.

Andrews, B. (1992). Attribution processes in victims of marital violence: Who do women blame and why? In J. H. Harvey, T. L. Orbuch, & A. L. Weber (Eds.), *Attributions, accounts, and close relationships* (pp. 177-193). New York: Springer-Verlag.

Baker, P. L. (1997). And I went back—Battered women's negotiations of choice. *Journal of Contemporary Ethnography, 26,* 55-74.

Becker, C. S. (1992). *Living and relating: An introduction to phenomenology.* Newbury Park, CA: Sage.

Bograd, M. (1984). Family systems approaches to wife battering: A feminist critique. *American Journal of Orthopsychiatry, 54,* 558-568.

Bograd, M. (1988). How battered women and abusive men account for domestic violence: Excuses, justifications, or explanations? In G. T. Hotaling, D. Finkelhor, J. T. Kirpatrik, & M. A. Straus (Eds.), *Coping with family violence: Research and policy perspectives* (pp. 60-77). Newbury Park, CA: Sage.

Bowker, L. H. (1993). A battered woman's problems are social, not psychological. In R. J. Gelles & D. R. Loseke (Eds.), *Current controversies on family violence* (pp. 154-165). Newbury Park, CA: Sage.

Browne, A. (1991). The victim's experience: Pathways to disclosure. *Psychotherapy, 28,* 150-156.

Campbell, J. C. (1995). *Assessing dangerousness: Violence by sexual offenders, batterers, and child abusers.* Thousand Oaks, CA: Sage.

Coleman, K. H. (1980). Conjugal violence: What 33 men report. *Journal of Marital and Family Therapy, 6,* 207-213.

Denzin, N. K. (1984). *On understanding emotion.* San Francisco: Jossey-Bass.

Denzin, N. K. (1989). *Interpretive interactionism.* Newbury Park, CA: Sage.

Dobash, R. E., & Dobash, R. P. (1990). How theoretical definitions and perspectives affect research and policy. In D. J. Besharov (Ed.), *Family violence: Research and public issues* (pp. 185-204). Washington, DC: AEI.

Duck, S. (1994). *Meaningful relationships: Talking, sense and relating.* Thousand Oaks, CA: Sage.

Dutton, D. G. (1988). *The domestic assault of women.* Boston: Allyn & Bacon.

Edleson, J. L., & Tolman, R. M. (1992). *Intervention for men who batter: An ecological approach.* Newbury Park, CA: Sage.

Efran, J. S., Lukens, R. J., & Lukens, M. D. (1988). Constructivism: What's in it for you. *The Family Therapy Networker, 12*(5), 27-35.

Eisikovits, Z. C., & Buchbinder, E. (1996). Toward a phenomenological intervention with violence in intimate relationships. In J. L. Edleson & Z. C. Eisikovits (Eds.), *Future interventions with battered women and their families* (pp. 186-200). Thousand Oaks, CA: Sage.

Eisikovits, Z. C., & Edleson, J. L. (1986). *Violence in the family: A study of men who batter.* A request to the Harry Guggenheim Foundation.

Eisikovits, Z., Goldblatt, H., & Winstok, Z. (1999). Partner accounts of intimate violence: Towards a theoretical model. *Families in Society, 80,* 606-619.

Ferraro, K. J. (1983). Rationalizing violence: How battered women stay. *Victimology, 8,* 203-212.

Gauthier, L. M., & Levendosky, A. A. (1996). Assessment and treatment of couples with abusive male partners: Guidelines for therapists. *Psychotherapy, 33,* 403-417.

Gergen, K. J. (1994). *Realities and relationships: Soundings in social construction.* Cambridge, MA: Harvard University Press.

Giles-Simms, J. (1983). *Wife battering: A systems theory approach.* New York: Guilford.

Goldblatt, H. (1997, March). *Filling the gaps: Accounting for emotions in spousal abuse.* Paper presented at the 7th International Conference on Family Therapy, Jerusalem.

Goldner, V. (1992, March/April). Making room for both/and. *The Family Therapy Networker, 16,* 55-61.

Gondolf, E. W. (1993). Treating the batterer. In M. Harway & M. Hansen (Eds.), *Battering and family therapy: A feminist perspective* (pp. 105-118). Newbury Park, CA: Sage.

Gondolf, E. W. (1998). *Assessing woman battering in mental health services.* Thousand Oaks, CA: Sage.

Gondolf, E. W., & Fisher, E. R. (1988). *Battered women as survivors: An alternative to treating learned helplessness.* Lexington, MA: Lexington Books.

Gondolf, E. W., & Hanneken, J. (1987). The gender warrior: Reformed batterers on abuse, treatment, and change. *Journal of Family Violence, 2,* 177-191.

Greenberg, L. S., & Pascual-Leone, J. (1997). Emotion in the creation of personal meaning. In M. Power & C. R. Brewin (Eds.), *The transformation of meaning in psychological therapies: Integrating theory and practice* (pp. 157-173). Chichester, UK: Wiley.

Guidano, V. F. (1995). Constructivist psychotherapy: A theoretical framework. In R. A. Neimeyer & M. J. Mahoney (Eds.), *Constructivism in psychotherapy* (pp. 93-108). Washington, DC: American Psychological Association.

Hansen, M. (1993). Feminism and family therapy: A review of feminist critiques of approaches to family violence. In M. Harway & M. Hansen (Eds.), *Battering and family therapy: A feminist perspective* (pp. 69-82). Newbury Park, CA: Sage.

Harway, M., & Hansen, M. (1993). Therapist perceptions of family violence. In M. Harway & M. Hansen (Eds.), *Battering and family therapy: A feminist perspective* (pp. 45-53). Newbury Park, CA: Sage.

Holtzworth-Munroe, A. (1992). Attributions and maritally violent men: The role of cognitions in marital violence. In J. H. Harvey, T. L. Orbuch, & A. L. Weber (Eds.), *Attributions, accounts, and close relationships* (pp. 165-175). New York: Springer-Verlag.

Hyden, M. (1994). *Woman battering as marital act: The construction of a violent marriage.* Oxford, UK: Scandinavian University Press.

Keen, S. (1992). *Fire in the belly: On being a man.* New York: Bantam.

Laing, R. D. (1960). *The divided self.* London: Tavistock.

Lincoln, Y. S., & Guba, E. G. (1985). *Naturalistic inquiry.* Beverly Hills, CA: Sage.

Linde, C. (1993). *Life stories: The creation of coherence.* New York: Oxford University Press.

Loewenberg, F., & Dolgoff, R. (1996). *Ethical decisions for social work practice* (5th ed.). Itasca, IL: F. E. Peacock.

Loseke, D. R. (1987). Realities and the construction of social problems: The case of wife abuse. *Symbolic Interaction, 10,* 224-243.

Loseke, D. R. (1991). Changing the boundaries of crime: The battered women's social movement and the definition of wife abuse as criminal activity. *Criminal Justice Review, 16,* 249-262.

Loseke, D. R., & Cahill, S. E. (1984). The social construction of deviance: Experts on battered women. *Social Problems, 31,* 296-310.

Margolin, G., & Burman, B. (1993). Wife abuse versus marital violence: Different terminologies, explanations, and solutions. *Clinical Psychology Review, 13,* 59-73.

Marris, P. (1980). The uprooting of meaning. In G. V. Goelho & P. I. Ahmed (Eds.), *Uprooting and development: Dilemmas of coping and modernalization* (pp. 101-116). New York: Plenum.

Mederer, H. J., & Gelles, R. J. (1989). Compassion or control: Intervention in cases of wife abuse. *Journal of Interpersonal Violence, 4,* 25-43.

Mullender, A. (1996). *Rethinking domestic abuse: The social work and the probation response.* London: Routledge.

Oxford English dictionary: The compact edition. (1971). New York: Oxford University Press.

Palmer, R. E. (1969). *Hermeneutics: Interpretation theory in Schleiermacher, Dilthey and Gadamer.* Evanston, IL: Northwestern University Press.

Potter, J. (1996). *Representing reality: Discourse, rhetoric and social construction.* London: Sage.

Profitt, N. J. (1996). "Battered women" as "victims" and "survivors": Creating a space for resistance. *Canadian Social Work Review, 13,* 23-38.

Ptacek, J. (1988). Why do men batter their wives? In K. Yllö & M. Bograd (Eds.), *Feminist perspectives on wife abuse* (pp. 133-157). Newbury Park, CA: Sage.

Register, E. (1993). Feminism and recovering from battering: Working with the individual woman. In M. Harway & M. Hansen (Eds.), *Battering and family therapy: A feminist perspective* (pp. 93-104). Newbury Park, CA: Sage.

Ricoeur, P. (1979). The model of the text: Meaningful action considered as a text. In P. Rabinow & W. M. Sullivan (Eds.), *Interpretive social science: A reader* (pp. 73-101). Berkeley: University of California Press.

Romanyshyn, R. D. (1982). *Psychological life: From science to metaphor.* Austin: University of Texas Press.

Sato, R. A. (1991). Assessment of the appropriateness of conjoint treatment with battering couples. *Advances in Family Intervention, Assessment and Theory, 5,* 69-88.

Schon, D. (1983). *The reflective practitioner: How professionals think in action.* New York: Basic Books.

Schutz, A. (1967). *The phenomenology of the social world.* Evanston, IL: Northwestern University Press.

Schwandt, T. A. (1994). Constructivist, interpretivist approaches to human inquiry. In K. Denzin & Y. S. Lincoln (Eds.), *Handbook of qualitative inquiry* (pp. 118-137). Thousand Oaks, CA: Sage.

Scott, M. B., & Lyman, S. M. (1968). Accounts. *American Sociological Review, 33,* 46-62.

Spinelli, E. (1997). *Tales of un-knowing: Eight stories of existential therapy.* New York: New York University Press.

Stamp, G. H., & Sabourin, T. C. (1995). Accounting for violence: An analysis of male spousal abuse narratives. *Journal of Applied Communication Research, 23,* 284-307.

Straus, M. A. (1996). Identifying offenders in criminal justice research on domestic assault. In E. S. Buzawa & C. G. Buzawa (Eds.), *Do arrests and restraining orders work?* (pp. 14-29). Thousand Oaks, CA: Sage.

Tolman, R. M. (1992). Psychological abuse of women. In R. T. Ammerman & M. Hersen (Eds.), *Assessment of family violence: A clinical and legal sourcebook* (pp. 291-310). New York: John Wiley.

Trute, B. (1998). Going beyond gender-specific treatments in wife battering: Pro-feminist couple and family therapy. *Aggression and Violent Behavior, 3,* 1-15.

Valle, R. S., & King, M. (1978). An introduction to existential-phenomenological thought in psychology. In R. S. Valle & M. King (Eds.), *Existential-phenomenological alternatives for psychology* (pp. 3-17). New York: Oxford University Press.

Walker, L. E. (1979). *The battered woman.* New York: Harper.

Walker, L. E. A. (1994). *Abused women and survivor therapy: A practical guide for the psychotherapist.* Washington, DC: American Psychological Association.

Widdershoven, G. A. M. (1993). The story of life: Hermeneutic perspectives on the relationship between narrative and life history. In R. Josselson & A. Lieblich (Eds.), *The narrative study of lives* (Vol. 1, pp. 1-20). Newbury Park, CA: Sage.

Yllö, K. A. (1993). Through a feminist lens: Gender, power, and violence. In R. J. Gelles & D. R. Loseke (Eds.), *Current controversies on family violence* (pp. 47-62). Newbury Park, CA: Sage.

Index

About the Authors

Zvi Eisikovits is a social worker and a criminologist. He was educated at the Hebrew University and received his PhD from the University of Minnesota in social work and youth studies. He is a professor of social work at the University of Haifa School of Social Work and director of the Minerva Center for Youth Studies at the university. His experience in social work includes working with youth in distress, gang work, administration of community centers in poor residential areas, and a series of consulting and policy activities ranging from national to local service development. During the last 15 years, he has been involved in developing national awareness to the plight of battered women and their children. He is the founding director of the Unit for Research and Intervention for Domestic Violence, a model agency that served as the basis for developing a network of similar services nationwide. He is presently conducting the first national survey in Israel on domestic violence and children at risk. His recent research includes a series of studies using a phenomenological perspective and addressing the insider's view of various aspects of intimate violence. He has published tens of articles and coedited edited three books in the areas of intimate violence and knowledge related to youth in distress. He is married; his wife, Rivka, is a professor of anthropology and education, and he has one adult son who is a doctoral student in law and philosophy.

Eli Buchbinder is a social worker and a doctoral student at the School of Social Work, The University of Haifa. His experience in social work includes a variety of populations and settings. He has worked with disturbed children in institutional settings, adolescent girls in distress, and couples and families in a couple and family therapy clinic and as a mental health officer in the army. He is one of the founders of the Unit for Research and Intervention for Domestic Violence, the first specialized unit working with domestic violence in Israel, where he has performed individual and group therapy with men who batter and survivors of violence. His experience also includes working with women and children in a battered women's shelter in Haifa. He specializes in qualitative research in the fields of domestic abuse, youth, and social workers' ways of knowing and professional socialization. He has published numerous articles and chapters in Hebrew and English, most of them with Zvi Eisikovits. He is presently working on his PhD dissertation on battered women's experience of their families of origin. He is married to Goldi, a teacher, and is the father of one daughter.